BUSINESS
COMES OF AGE

Karl Schriftgiesser

BUSINESS
COMES OF AGE

The Story of the Committee
for Economic Development
and Its Impact upon the Economic Policies of the United
States, 1942–1960.

Harper & Brothers
Publishers New York

BUSINESS COMES OF AGE

Library of Congress catalog card number: 60–5709

CONTENTS

v

PREFACE

AMONG BUSINESS organizations and institutions, of which there are many thousands in the United States, the Committee for Economic Development occupies a unique place. Familiarly known as CED, the initials of this committee appear often in the headlines, on the radio, and televised newscasts. Its infrequent but always authoritative and often controversial pronunciamentos are grist for editorial writers, columnists, and other journalistic pundits who recognize its statements on national economic policy as the considered judgment of a small but powerful segment of the business community.

To most of those who are familiar with its utterances CED represents the more progressive and liberal wing of Big Business. For seventeen years what it says and the way it says it have commanded the respect of professional economists and other social scientists, who have long been aware of the unusual character of the process whereby CED arrives at its conclusions on economic and social problems. But to the general public, in spite of the fact that it has played a decidedly important role in the economic history of this country since World War II, CED is not as well known as it might be.

Many people, recalling the stimulating role it played in planning during the war to prevent a postwar depression, confuse its initials with a government agency, although from its beginning it has had no official connection with the federal government. Too few realize that CED is not a manufacturers' association, not a chamber of commerce, not a trade association, not even an endowed foundation. They are unaware of the fact that it is an unusual—indeed, unique—combination of businessmen and industrialists who work with scholars from the great universities in a joint effort of economic research and policy making.

CED was the first such organization in the United States, probably in the world. Its sole aim is to arrive through conscientious and objective study at economic policies within the framework of our free enterprise system and our democratic form of government which will redound to the benefit of the general welfare through maintaining high employment and economic stability.

The history of CED is the story of an unusual intellectual experiment in the business community of America—a merging of the best minds from the most successful corporations and the best universities in this common effort. This book tells how this institution came into being at the start of World War II, what it did in a major effort to avert a postwar recession, and how it evolved into its present highly respected position as the mouthpiece of business intelligence. It tells of CED's successes—the salvaging of the Bretton Woods agreements and the passage of the Employment Act of 1946, for examples—and of its failures. It describes the origin and development of its historic stabilizing budget policy and flexible monetary policy. And it shows, I hope, the impact CED has had upon the economic thinking of the United States from 1942 to the present.

Perhaps the most exciting story that it tells is of the emergence of the American businessman from the doghouse into which he had jammed himself almost inextricably in the years of normalcy, Calvin Coolidge, and Herbert Hoover, through the catharsis of the New Deal and the Fair Deal, to his present accepted status within our democratic society. Hence its title, *Business Comes of Age,* for in this historic process CED played a major if sometimes lonely part.

In the preparation of this book I have had the fullest cooperation of the CED—its board of trustees, officers, and staff. However, my arrangement with CED was that I should have the fullest freedom. This is not, then, an "official" history of CED, but my own independent interpretation. The opinions expressed herein are my own. The errors of judgment (and of fact) that may have crept in are my responsibility.

I should like to express my thanks to CED's trustees for this freedom. I should like to mention the following who were most generous with their time and material: Messrs. Paul G. Hoffman, William Benton, Ralph Flanders, Harry Scherman, Thomas B. McCabe, Wayne C. Taylor, Donald K. David, J. D. Zellerbach, Frazar B. Wilde, Howard Petersen, and J. Cameron Thomson; Theodore Schultz, Calvin B. Hoover, Neil H. Jacoby, and Herbert Stein; Robert H. Lenhart, Alfred C. Neal, Porter McKeever, Herbert Malley, Miss Mary Mugivan, and Miss Matilda Tobias. And a special word of gratitude goes to Mrs. Ruth Cobbett Biemiller of the *New York Herald Tribune.*

K. S.

ONE

Discovering the General Welfare

In 1941, that fateful year which ended with the date that will live in infamy, the eight-year struggle of the New Deal to rehabilitate the American way of life, was ended. But those eight years had been electric.

Every American knew that in some way his life had been changed. Perhaps that amorphous creature known as the American businessman realized it better than anyone, for whether he was George Babbitt of Main Street or a money changer in the temples of Wall Street, he had been near the center of the change. Many strange things had happened to the capitalism of which he was the core. The old and sacred private-profit, individual-enterprise system had been shocked as never before.

What, exactly, had taken place in the great democracy, the old America, the land of opportunity, in those bewildering years? It was, at the start of 1941, hard to say. Had the New Deal succeeded in reaching its aims, or had it failed? And what, precisely, were those aims?

If relief of the vast army of the unemployed had been its major goal, then it had succeeded, for it had kept a starving, frightened multitude from disaster through direct relief and the use of public works. If the future security of the people was its goal,

1

then it had not failed, for nearly one-half the nation's working force now had some measure of social security. If alleviating the lot of the farmers, homeowners, and slum dwellers was its goal, then it had at least changed the national thinking and made it clear that such matters were a national and not a local concern.

The New Deal, so vigorously assailed as destructive of our economic system, had tightened if not wholly mended the loose banking system of the country. It had rebuked and restrained the huge and harmful holding companies that had played so tragic a part in the national disaster. It had curbed the frauds who had infested the stock exchanges. And it had brought recognition in law and in practice to organized labor.

All the profound economic innovations, those that worked and those that did not, added up to a new doctrine that had been slowly in the making throughout the history of the republic. This doctrine was simple: that the federal government could and should act as an economic balance wheel. This was made a certainty in the 1930's, against the concerted, sometimes hysterical, always vigorous opposition of business and its spokesmen. Only the NRA which, had it not been found unconstitutional, might well have wrecked the free, competitive system through its anticompetitive codes of self-regulation, aroused the enthusiasm of the business community.

Years later the magazine of the business elite, *Fortune*, looked back upon this time and said, "The basic reason the depression lasted so long was the economic ignorance of the times." This ignorance was not confined to "that man in the White House." It permeated the business community. It expressed itself in the blind worship by business of the ideal of the balanced budget, the fear of deficits, the hatred of governmental intervention. It was not until ten years after the New Deal had begun that a business organization recognized and espoused the theory that the government has at all times the positive obligation to keep the national economy stable and in forward motion.

It is true, of course, that, more than once in its search for economic safety, the New Deal had chased its own tail. It had attempted inflation—and then turned to price controls. A policy of profuse government spending had been followed by stern restrictions, only for it to turn again to government spending. It had thrown aside the antitrust laws to allow a vast system of business collusion, only to launch, but never prosecute, a program of trust-busting. It had wooed, and then spurned, economic nationalism.

Although, at the end of 1939, there were still between 8 and 9 million unemployed persons in the country, the New Deal had done one thing that, perhaps, was more important than anything else. It had restored national morale and established a higher order of social justice than its generation had known. It had changed the direction of American thinking. In a sense it had given new and lasting meaning to the words of the Constitution; by 1941 the words "general welfare" had sunk into the American consciousness with a meaning probably far beyond that of its authors. One did not have to be a New Dealer to understand this. It was history now and an accomplished fact.

The business community, however, still seemed to live in an atmosphere of McKinleyism. The social philosophy of Mark Hanna's era, so succinctly expressed by the economist Frank Albert Fetter in 1891, still seemed to be the maxim of too many business leaders: "Self, self, self is the axiom of evolution, the postulate of political economy, the rule of human action."

But now that war threatened to engulf all Europe and spread to American shores, another change in national thinking occurred, especially in the business community. As war orders began pouring in upon industry and as the American defense effort accelerated, it became necessary for business to become the active partner instead of the suspicious protégé or hostile observer of the government.

Nevertheless, as one acute observer of those times put it, for some time vocal businessmen were inclined to refuse to be wooed by Washington. They feared the Greeks though bearing gifts.

Many thought that preparations for war, or even war itself, would intensify dreaded governmental power and control over their private enterprises. Many of them, cringing in isolation, were certain that the temporary wartime prosperity would end in worse disaster than that of 1929.

Important industrialists wavered. The jeers against the sit-down strike of capital were justified. But eventually, when it began to dawn that the government was ready to assume the major financial risks if they would but accept defense orders, they forgot their old ideological fears. They expanded their plants and revved up their machines. When help was offered through RFC, and cost-plus contracts and carry-back of losses, they rolled up their sleeves with a will.

Then America went to war.

While the hugest industrial plant in history, the great "arsenal of democracy," was grinding away at full blast and America's sons were fighting and dying on two strange continents, much thinking was going on in the nation about the future, the brave new world that was to be after the war.

On many fronts planners were planning for this future with one thing in mind. This was the simple postulate that—since anything but victory on the battlefield was unthinkable—America must be prepared for peace. There must be no economic breakdown this time, no financial debacle, no industrial collapse.

In government offices this planning occupied many minds. Some of the planners unquestionably intended to extend the wartime power of government over business and industry, over prices and wages, so that, through such rigid controls, private enterprise would be coerced into the extremes of a welfare state. Driven by the specter of vast armies of unemployed, of darkened factories, and shuttered stores, they were determined to make every use of governmental power to avoid economic collapse.

In the business community there was indifference—except among a few who had not forgotten, in the stress of wartime, the lessons of the eleven-year depression that had only begun to disappear when Pearl Harbor fell.

These few remembered that unemployment had soared from a rate of 9 per cent in the first year to a high of 25 per cent in the worst year and that during eight years one out of every five wage earners had been jobless.

These few were determined that this should not happen again. They were not frightened by the word *planning*. They did not accept as gospel the 1915 dictum of the sociologist, Graham Taylor, when he said that "the only thing men really plan for is war." Man could, if he would, plan also for peace—and for prosperity as well.

These few men were unusual inhabitants of the business community. They had been neither scared nor soured by the New Deal. They realized, as many of their frightened contemporaries did not, that the upheavals of the 1930's had been both necessary and inevitable if the social, political, industrial, and financial institutions were not to enter a period of decay.

These men knew, if only imperfectly, that great changes had been going on in the American economy for nearly half a century and that vast national economic adjustments had been taking place. They knew that our social standards were no longer those of McKinley's day and that our financial institutions were not the same as those which had disturbed Senator Aldrich. They knew that the reforms of Theodore Roosevelt and the "new freedom" of Woodrow Wilson had fundamentally changed the economic structure of the United States long before Franklin Delano Roosevelt changed them even more.

They knew, or suspected, that the great problem of the future was finding ways and means of preserving and strengthening the good habits and sound institutions of the American economic system that had sprung through trial and error in times of trouble from the common sense of the American people.

Profound believers in democracy and in the private enterprise system, they were not afraid of government or of the power of politics over economic trends. Believers in economic growth, they were also believers in the general welfare, which could be translated to mean high employment and high productivity, which also meant, in their interpretation, high standards of living for all the people.

Attainment of such high goals, they understood, would not be an easy task. Before they could be reached there were immediate problems to be solved. Of these the most pressing was to convince the business community that it was the duty of private enterprise to find its own way to a smooth transition from a wartime economy to a peacetime economy. In order to do this the business community must start planning and keep on planning, no matter how far away, or how unsure, that peacetime might seem to be.

At the same time that thinking in this direction was being done by a woefully small segment of the businessmen of America, the idea of a national organization of businessmen, independent of government yet working closely with it toward the goal of thwarting a postwar economic collapse through careful planning, was being nurtured in the United States Department of Commerce under Secretary Jesse Jones. In 1942, a few months after Pearl Harbor, he sent out his call to action.

Quite independently, two other men had been working on a different scheme which now was to be a significant factor in the success of Jesse Jones's plan. For several years Paul G. Hoffman and William Benton had been talking about bringing together outstanding businessmen and industrialists into a close working alliance with the best economists and social scientists the great universities of the country could supply. They believed that by bringing these men of action and these men of thought into a sort of national seminar, great advances could be made toward a practical understanding of the rapidly changing economic complexities of our time. How these two ideas were brought together is an exciting chapter in the business history of the United States.

When Benton and Hoffman were planning their organization

they had three purposes in mind. One, and to them perhaps the most important, was to rescue the businessman from his own intellectual neanderthalism, to wash the clichés of an outworn ideology from his mind. They wanted to make him more understanding of and responsive to the broad sweep of economic thinking which lay behind the political, social, and economic upheavals that had been occurring at such a rapid rate throughout most of the twentieth century.

At the same time they wanted to bring the academicians and their theories into free association with men who had risen to commanding positions in industry and business, hopeful that such contact would wipe the theoretical cobwebs from thinkers' minds.

The third purpose was to guide the leaders of business and industry, with the best aid possible from the academicians, into positions where their contributions to the making of national economic policy would be validly offered and received.

In order to do this they envisaged the utilization of scientific research on a broad scale, hopeful that the results thus attained might lead to better understanding of the economic problems facing legislatures, administrators, and the people.

In a world that had rudely changed even before the destructive force of World War II had fallen, deeper and better and more imaginative knowledge of every facet of economic thinking was needed. Economic education on every level was the hope of a better life.

It was needed, these two men thought, if our private enterprise system was to continue to work within the democratic tradition, both of which had together made America the great world power it had suddenly become. The economic growth of the country and the general welfare of its citizens demanded it. There could be no question of turning the clock back to isolationism and *laissez faire*.

From the economic thinkers of the past half century, before and after Lord Keynes, had come tools that could be used to build an economic stability such as the world had never before known. To find how to put these tools to use and to discover other tools not yet invented, were the great postwar tasks facing both business and government.

This is a story that needs telling, for it is a story of a great intellectual drama played out within the business community where enlightened and progressive thought has not always been noticeable. It is a part of the economic history of our time.

TWO

After Victory, What?

AGAINST A background of great economic uncertainty, three men came together on the campus of the University of Chicago on an early spring day in 1941. They were the youthful and ebullient Dr. Robert M. Hutchins, president of the University, Paul G. Hoffman, president of the Studebaker Company, and William Benton, a brilliant young advertising man who had sold his share in the Madison Avenue firm of Benton and Bowles to become the University's vice-president.

Although William Benton had spent most of his life as what the irreverent called a "huckster," and Paul Hoffman had spent his selling automobiles, they were both essentially thinking men. In his years as industrialist and salesman, Paul Hoffman had become deeply concerned about the functioning of democracy. He had arrived painfully at the conclusion that industrial problems could not be separated from social and political problems, much as adherents of old-fashioned *laissez faire*, vocally at least, might wish them to be. William Benton, whose adventures in advertising had brought him into close contact with a wide variety of industries and businesses and their leaders, was equally concerned.

For some time Hoffman, despite his major preoccupation

with rebuilding the Studebaker Company, had been troubled by what he believed was the most serious economic problem facing the country. Nothing either industry or government had attempted had yet succeeded in doing away with the curse of widespread unemployment. Even with the lift which the outbreak of war in Europe had given, American industry had been able to absorb less than one-half million from the idle labor force in more than a year. Many of his friends in industry were convinced that the free economy of which this country boasted would never find the answer. To him this was an ominous thought. The more he pondered the more he wondered whether, if it were approached objectively, without regard to politics and in a scientific manner, some lasting answers might not be found.

Since coming to the University Benton, too, had thought in a somewhat similar direction. Although he had studied economics at Yale and had a better than average understanding of business practices, he was astonished to discover how ignorant he was of the forces that made the economy work—or kept it from working. His new association with the academic mind—and the University of Chicago had, at that time, one of the most vigorous economics faculties in the country—had impressed him with what seemed to him an abysmal waste of talent. He was astonished that business was making little palpable use of the brains it might so easily command.

Stimulated by the professors with whom he was in frequent contact, a few years before the campus meeting Benton had approached an old friend, Lewis Brown, president of Johns Manville Company, with a novel idea. Benton told his friend that the persons who most needed an education in economics were the presidents of America's one hundred largest corporations. If these gentlemen could be brought into active contact with the country's best economists in a series of week-end "classes" he was sure that both industry and the country would benefit. Brown was impressed and the pair had several conversations. But the outbreak of war in Europe in 1939 delayed Benton in carrying out the idea.

As the three men conferred on the Chicago campus, Hoffman stated his view this way:

"As a trustee of the university I think it's high time the university played a more active role in trying to do something about the state of the nation. The University of Chicago has economists and other scholars. These men have the knowledge, but their knowledge is not being applied to the good of the country. What can we do about it?"

Hoffman continued: "After ten years of struggle America still has 8 million unemployed. Unemployment is a social disease gnawing at our vitals. High levels of production are the only cure for unemployment and the only road to national health.

"Here is a problem for university scholars. Their knowledge and the knowledge of businessmen who understand the nature of this problem must be brought together. . . ."

Having startled his companions, who shared the impression that the University of Chicago for fifty years had been contributing its part in improving the state of the nation through education, Hoffman elaborated upon the plan he had in mind.

He proposed a study on "what is the matter with democracy—an analysis of practices of business which are harmful to democracy; of education; of the church; of labor." To make this study he would set up a committee of twenty or twenty-five businessmen, labor leaders, churchmen, and so on, "chosen with the view of making constructive contributions." He proposed to engage a researcher to work with this group, under the auspices of the University of Chicago, who would act as counselor and guide.

Both the university president and the former advertising man were moved by Hoffman's plea. The very next day Benton began to work on the project. In a letter to a potential research director he wrote:

"Hoffman thinks that a frank analysis, under such auspices, might do a great deal to illuminate the opinion of influential groups in this country, thus giving the country a much better chance to correct abuses and to keep democracy at work."

To Dr. Hutchins, Hoffman's words were a challenge to the University; to Benton they gave a chance to revive the idea with which he and Lewis Brown had toyed many months before.

Within a few weeks Benton and Hoffman were deep in plans for establishing a group which they intended to call the American Policy Commission. As they worked it out in many conferences, this was to be a combination of Benton's original idea and the *Fortune* Round Table, which had been started in 1939. The Round Table brought together such men as Sumner Slichter, the Harvard economist, the heads of the New Jersey Bell Telephone Company, the Detroit Edison Company, and a leading engineering firm, a federal judge from Georgia, and an Iowa farmer, for informal, unprepared discussions of such pressing problems as "the effect of government spending on private enterprise."

Apparently the evolving scheme eliminated labor leaders, farmers, and churchmen and was restricted to business leaders only, as in Benton's early idea, although these were not to be confined to corporation presidents. It was now planned to assemble fifteen or twenty "literate businessmen"—Benton's words —who would be willing to "devote time, effort, energy and money," at two- and three-day sessions to be held four or six times a year. At these meetings they would thrash out answers to questions of public policy. Working with them would be economists and other scientists from the staff of the University of Chicago. These businessmen were to be picked for their understanding of national problems and not for their names. The same men would meet each time, "learning," as Benton put it, "as they went along." Unlike the Round Table participants, they would be prepared for each meeting through personal interviews with economists and social scientists and through "homework" with memoranda especially prepared by academic experts who would be brought in from business, government, and the universities. At the end of each six months the joint conclusions of the business and academic group would be published.

In the following weeks William Benton threw himself energetically into organizing the American Policy Commission. Both he and Hoffman approached many carefully selected businessmen with their idea. They sought out such men as Ralph Flanders, the Vermont toolmaker and Boston banker; Thomas B. McCabe, head of the Scott Paper Company; Henry Luce of *Life*, *Time*, and *Fortune*; Marshall Field, the Chicago storekeeper and newspaper publisher; Clarence Francis, head of General Foods; Ray Rubicam, the advertising man; Beardsley Ruml, economic planner, treasurer of Macy's, and former dean of social sciences at Chicago; R. R. Deupree of Procter and Gamble; and Fowler McCormick.

In the course of several months spent in writing, talking, flying planes, and riding trains around the country, the American Policy Commission was beginning to take a definite shape. Then the bombs fell on Pearl Harbor.

As millions of youths went into the Armed Forces and other millions, old and young, men and women, joined the huge labor force that soon was to seem all but inadequate to meet the demands of the nation and its allies, there were some, both in and out of the government, who were already thinking about the problems of the hoped-for peace.

Within the Department of Commerce in Washington and in some other federal departments—notably the ill-fated National Resources Planning Board, whose report, *After Defense, What?*, was published in 1945—the problems of postwar planning were being considered even before the United States had declared war. There was a strong determination, at least among some of the New Deal "bureaucrats" and, as we shall see, among some enlightened businessmen, that the American economy should not be thrown into a disastrous tailspin when war ended. Remembering what had happened after World War I—when, many economists believed, the seeds of trouble that sprouted in 1929 were sown—they were convinced that only through conscientious planning and the working out of definite programs could a salutary transition from a war to a peacetime economy be managed.

The coming of war had quickly taught one lesson—that government and business *could* work together. The huge increases in the working force, the enormous expansion of the industrial plant, made it obvious that this cooperation must continue when the war was over and war orders, on which American business and industry were concentrating all their energies, ceased. When this time came—and, as in all wars, it was generally recognized that it might come suddenly—the return of thousands of troops and the quick cancellation of contracts, coming together, would force upon America another paralyzing period of confusion, with crippling unemployment everywhere. There were some who said openly that there would be 30 million Americans out of work and that the worst depression in history would sweep the land.

As Thomas B. McCabe, who was to play an important part in the businessman's crusade for a better postwar world, said later, in recalling these days:

"We were still close to the days of the early Thirties, when stagnation and unemployment were rampant. We knew we dared not face another period of unemployment like that. And we knew that if we did the chances for our way of life were dim. We determined to put everything we had into an effort to avoid that calamity. . . . We knew that Government would have to play its part, probably the major part. . . ."

To a small group in the Department of Commerce, then under the businesslike rule of the redoubtable Jesse Jones of Texas, the cooperative attitude of men like McCabe was a blessing. Since the Department was by law charged with the duty of promoting and fostering commerce and industry, it welcomed intelligent outside encouragement from that powerful source.

The fear of a return to the stagnant, wasteful thirties was

general. In labor, intellectual, and political circles a great deal of attention was being paid, in these days, to often fearful thinking about what the world would be like after the war. There was a grim determination that it should not be a world of retrogression, that the war against fascism was not being fought to allow the world to slip backward but to cleanse the atmosphere for a bright new dawn. The Four Freedoms were being taken seriously.

And so the phrase "postwar planning" crept into the language. At first business in general did not take kindly to it. The word "planning" smacked of New Dealism, creeping socialism, or worse. But within the government there were serious and conscientious, if not coordinated, efforts to focus attention upon the problems which would face the country when the fighting stopped. Especially did those officials who were concerned primarily with the economic aspects of government take the challenge of the future seriously. And they turned their minds in this direction long before Pearl Harbor, for they were aware, nearly a year before the United States was forced into the war, that the huge spending for defense was creating a lasting change in our entire industrial economy.

The Department of Commerce became involved in postwar planning at least as early as August, 1941. At about the time President Roosevelt and Prime Minister Churchill were conferring at sea aboard U.S.S. *Augusta*, a new unit was set up within the department. Known as the National Economics Unit, it was a part of the Bureau of Foreign and Domestic Commerce and was headed by Arthur R. Upgren.

At the suggestion of Carroll Wilson, director of the Bureau of Foreign and Domestic Commerce, and M. Joseph Meehan, chief of the Division of Research and Statistics, the four-man Economics Unit began searching for an effective program for that potentially dangerous period when war-fed industry would be thrown back on its own resources. By early November, while Congress was bitterly debating revisions of the Neutrality Act,

Upgren was engaged in working up a draft of such a plan. At the same time other Department of Commerce statisticians were gathering data for what was to become its famous report, *Markets After the War*.

As a result of this activity, Wilson and Meehan became convinced that private enterprise could close the gap when, as the saying then went, "Uncle Sam stops paying $100 billion a year for war." But they realized that if this were to be accomplished there would have to be some kind of citizens' businessman's organization with which the Department of Commerce could work in finding ways to this goal.

During the autumn of 1941, Upgren was assigned to explore the possibilities of organizing such a committee. Less than a month after Pearl Harbor he and his associate, Richard M. Bissell, submitted their first report, *A Program of Postwar Planning*. It contained specific recommendations as to how the private sector of the economy could work with government when the time came.

Constructive concern for the future of private enterprise was more evident in government than in business. Businessmen were too busily engaged in the competitive struggle of capturing their share of the activity financed by government funds to interest themselves in planning for the day when those funds would cease to flow. Among the nation's largest industrial corporations there was only one notable exception, General Electric, which already had worked out estimates of future demand for its products under a variety of possible circumstances, had made preliminary decisions as to what its capital expenditures should be in the future, and had started to determine how its plants could most effectively be converted from all-out war production to peacetime use.

Basing his report to some extent on the work of General Electric, Upgren recommended two steps for the business community. First, each company should forecast as well as possible the demand for consumers' goods and opportunities for private investment, on the assumption that the level of the national income would be maintained. Second, each company should begin at once to prepare for readjustments and capital expenditures that their forecasts indicated would be necessary.

In the light of future developments the key paragraph of his report was: "If the evidence [deduced from such research] suggested that the dominant problem after the war would be that of avoiding stagnation and maintaining full employment, then the emphasis should be placed on planning a shelf of *private* projects, which can be initiated when the situation demands." Although none knew it at this time, the idea of Benton and Hoffman had moved a step nearer its goal.

Meanwhile the Department of Commerce continued its exploratory work through meetings with leading businessmen in New York and Washington, with the Bureau of Labor Statistics, and the National Resources Planning Board, both of which were also busy with postwar plans. Arthur Upgren also talked with representatives of the Rockefeller Foundation and the Social Sciences Research Council, who were ready to offer their cooperation, and possibly some financial support.

As a result of his conferences, Upgren discovered that "no attempt is yet being made either to direct and organize whatever work is now being done outside the Government or to stimulate activity on a wider scale. . . . Doubtless, as the war progresses, more and more planning for the private sector will be done, in other Federal Agencies, in communities which approach the matter from a regional point of view, in individual firms. . . . But there is no guarantee that its implications for the economy as a whole will be developed."

The lack of leadership in the private sector was depressing. As far as Upgren could discover, David W. Prince of General Electric was almost alone in sensing, and in urging his industrial associates to realize, the need for coordinated effort. Others, of course, were seriously concerned about this problem, but they were working in a vacuum. What was needed, as the Department of Commerce investigation was showing, was some way to create an all-out national, industrial program that would bring together all segments of business and industry under a master plan.

Upgren's report recommended that the Bureau of Domestic and Foreign Commerce "take steps immediately to secure the setting up of a committee which can stimulate and, in some measure, direct a broad investigation of postwar private investment opportunities." It seemed up to the Department of Commerce to make the first moves as, at that time, there seemed to be "no other organization, public or private, prepared to take the lead."

Those closely associated with the project were convinced that the proposed investigations should not be conducted by the United States Chamber of Commerce, the National Association of Manufacturers, or any trade or industry organization, because, as Upgren put it, "the impartiality of the research must be above question, which it certainly would not be if it were conducted by official spokesmen for business."

Undersecretary of Commerce Wayne Chatfield Taylor, who was soon to undertake the task of coordinating the proposed investigation, was insistent upon what he called "quasi-independence" for the committee. Only this status would provide the needed assurance that the "organized effort of the business community would serve a national and not a narrow business interest."

At this early stage it was recommended that the investigation and planning be conducted by businessmen, with the Commerce Department supplying the technical staff and acting as a connecting link between all public planning then in progress in the many governmental agencies and the private planning that, it was hoped, the cooperative efforts would encourage. The government officials were reluctant, however, for the Commerce Department to become too deeply involved. They were convinced that the plan would be a failure if the business community, as one of them said, were not "forced to face up to the problems." Also, they felt that overt Commerce Department involvement would discourage the cooperation of the business community and that business would cavalierly dismiss it as "just another New Deal plan."

This concern was born of hard experience. Back in 1933, Secretary of Commerce Roper had invited representative business leaders to serve in an advisory capacity to the President and the Secretary of Commerce with respect, particularly, to governmental policies affecting business. But many businessmen had persistently regarded this Business Advisory Council with suspicion. Many looked upon it as a trap and more generous ones treated it as mere dressing for unpalatable New Deal policies.

Yet the "Roper Committee," as some businessmen derisively referred to it, had struggled on and in the autumn of 1941 some of its members called upon Undersecretary Taylor to protest that certain recent reports on postwar planning by the National Resources Planning Board had "neglected business and industry." They were, Mr. Taylor recalls, "quite mad."

"No one in government asks us what business's postwar plans are," one member complained.

"That's probably because you have none," Mr. Taylor replied. Nor did they.

This situation, however, soon changed. When the Commerce Department's plan was presented to the members of the Business Advisory Council, with the full approval of Secretary Jones, they were ready for it and extended cooperation that was indispensable to the success of the project.

Fortunately the Economic Policy Committee of the Business Advisory Council, with which early consultations were held, was headed by Marion B. Folsom. The Georgia-born Folsom, then but forty-seven years old, who had gone from the Harvard Graduate School of Business Administration to Eastman Kodak Company at the age of twenty-one, was at this time treasurer of the multimillion-dollar company. He was best known as creator of the Eastman pension plan and the Rochester Unemployment Plan. The latter, started right after the crash of 1929, was a pioneer study of the problem of stabilizing production and unemployment, which had had concrete results. President Roosevelt, in 1934, had called him to his Advisory Council on Economic Security, and he had been a delegate in 1936 to the International Labor Conference at Geneva, Switzerland. As a member, 1937–1938, of the federal Advisory Council on Social Security, he had contributed materially to one of the New Deal's most lasting social experiments.

As a businessman who had active experience in the government, probably few men on the Washington scene in 1941 were more acutely aware than Folsom of the problems that would face the postwar world. He was quick to see merit in the department's project and quick, too, to see some of its inherent faults. He had a long talk with Jesse Jones and told him that some sort of businessmen's committee, designed to stimulate postwar high employment, was necessary. Nobody was more in agreement than Jesse Jones. With Folsom's assurance of cooperation and Jones's approval, the plan began to move ahead at high speed.

A formal session of the Business Advisory Council was called in late January, 1942, to hear Carroll Wilson outline the proposal as it had been beaten out and modified in many department meetings. The huge size of the program, which would affect almost every business in the country, and the basic necessity of cooperation on a national, regional, and local scale, were stressed in Wilson's report. It foresaw an all-out effort on the part of business, one that would take time, money, patriotism, and brains to accomplish.

In detail the plan called for every enterprise, commercial or industrial, large or small, to make its own estimate, in tangible, quantitative terms, of the markets that—assuming the continuance of full employment and high production—would be open when wartime restrictions were lifted. Once this was determined, comprehensive and specific plans were to be made for the investments that would be necessary to exploit these markets. With this an appraisal of investment risks was to be made.

In order to create such a plan, the management of each enterprise, of whatever size, would require information and assistance outside its own business and, in turn, would have to furnish information of its own plans to help others. Through this cooperative gathering of statistics on forthcoming demand (under conditions of high employment and productivity) the *over-all demand* for postwar America would be revealed, and business would have a goal to aim at.

To know "what the score was," each individual management would have to have available estimates of the anticipated sales, plans for new equipment, and construction of new facilities, of every business affecting his own. For, in the dusty governmental words of the old report, "in appraising the prospective risks of investment each enterprise will require specific assurance that a flow of customer orders is going to energize and maintain the level of employment." And since "the full employment market" that was anticipated would appear only if national production of consumers' goods, houses, and capital goods was kept at a high rate, then each management would have to be assured that all the other managements were planning to produce and expand on a scale that would guarantee such a market.

The magnitude of the task envisaged was such that the Commerce Department, itself already beset by wartime burdens and faced with a manpower shortage, could not assume full responsibility. And so it asked for the creation, as soon as possible (because none knew how long the war would last and the task would be time-consuming no matter how well-organized), of a permanent committee of "outstanding business authorities who are also public-spirited citizens" to step in and do the job. The Department of Commerce would, however, supply technical assistance and advice. It was suggested that a budget of not less than $50,000 for the first year would be sufficient, especially if, as was hoped, a substantial number of leading enterprises would assign competent personnel to the preparation of their own post-war plans and to work with the committee.

With this definite proposal laid before the Business Advisory Council things began to hum. Many meetings held between January and May advanced the progress of what for want of a better name was then generally referred to as the "Bureau of Business Enterprise." Undersecretary Taylor and Walter White, the executive secretary of the BAC, came to the conclusion that the BAC was the body to do the job. Then followed several conferences with officials of the National Association of Manufacturers and the Chamber of Commerce. These gentlemen realized the necessity of the proposed organization but backed away from active participation or direction.

As Benton later recalled this situation, "They agreed that the problem of employment after the war was so urgent that no present business organization was equipped to do justice to it. They agreed further that a new business organization should be formed with high levels of post-war employment as its sole objective." But it really was not quite as simple as this may seem. Neither of the old established business organizations had any intention of allowing a permanent rival to creep onto the scene. In later conferences with Secretary Jones, the Chamber and the NAM exacted a so-called "gentleman's agreement" to the effect that any organization of the kind proposed should be set up for the duration of the war only. Once its immediate postwar objectives had been achieved it was to be dissolved. This solemn but unwritten pact was to cause some difficulties in later years.

However, at the time these discussions were taking place the research program, which Hoffman was to insist upon as an integral part of the committee's function, had not been worked out or accepted by Secretary Jones. As far as the National Association of Manufacturers and the United States Chamber of Commerce were then concerned, the proposed organization was to concern itself exclusively with the problems that would face business and industry in the period immediately following the end of the war, and certainly not with long-range economic policies.

In the meantime Paul Hoffman and Marion B. Folsom had come together for a series of serious discussions and Hoffman had shown a keen interest in the proposal. In the second week in May, Secretary Jones called a select group of businessmen to his office. Folsom and Hoffman were among those who listened to him describe the plan in terms very similar to those which Carroll Wilson had outlined in January to the Business Advisory Council.

At this time Benton, who was still hopeful that he might carry through his American Policy Commission, was working on a scheme whereby the University of Chicago and two other leading institutions would make a study of postwar potentialities for the American economy. He even had a conference on this subject in Washington with former President Herbert C. Hoover. Now, two or three days after the meeting in Secretary Jones's office, Hoffman sent Benton to see Folsom. In this conference, which lasted two hours, Benton suggested "that our group [apparently he meant the proposed nucleus of American Policy Commission] be incorporated into his [Jesse Jones's] key committee, as half of the people we were considering he wanted anyway and the other half are suitable. Then our group could be set up as a sub-committee on long-range planning."

Benton reported back to Hoffman and told him what he had suggested. The following week end Hoffman met with Folsom, whom Benton had found "one of the smartest and most stimulating fellows I have met in a long time." Hoffman, who was by now very enthusiastic about combining the two ideas, found Folsom was opposed to research per se, although he had known full well its basic value both in the Eastman laboratories and in his own sociological experiments in Rochester. But he did not then see clearly the value of combining long-range research with what he conceived to be fundamentally a propaganda machine formed to spread the necessity of practical, plant-by-plant thinking about industrial postwar planning.

Undeterred by Folsom's reaction, Hoffman and Benton together called on Secretary Jones. Well aware of the Texan's reputation as a coldly thinking, pragmatic businessman they were prepared for disappointment. "Mr. Hoffman made an essential requirement of our acceptance [of positions on the proposed committee] the launching of an objective research program into public policy. Hoffman described in broad outline a program challenging policies of labor, business, agriculture, and government which would work against the attainment of high levels of employment and production."

Secretary Jones listened intently and then asked, "Well, boys, what would you study?" Hoffman gave a number of concrete examples, stressing taxation and the hodgepodge of federal tax laws.

"All right," the Secretary replied. "It sounds practical to me."

When Hoffman said that the proposed committee should be prepared to spend as much as 50 per cent of its budget on this research program, Jones again said, "It sounds practical to me."

"It was," Benton said afterward, "our easiest sale."

By this time Secretary Jones, assured of staunch business support, had taken over wholehearted control of the program. From his office he directed the key appointments that were to give the organization solidity. Although some New Dealers looked upon the Secretary as an ultraconservative, and some businessmen found him suspect because he was in Roosevelt's corner, he held, in general, the respect of businessmen everywhere. His acquaintance with leading businessmen and bankers in every corner of the nation was phenomenal. He could pick up the phone and call at least one man he knew and trusted in almost every city or town anywhere. His persuasiveness was as legendary as his laconic speech. His telephone was busy many hours of the day now, as singlehandedly he recruited all the original membership. Although he took suggestions from others, his was the final decision and every person associated with the new organization was his personal choice.

Among those suggested by Hoffman and Benton for the original board of trustees were Ralph Flanders, Thomas B. McCabe, Henry Luce, Marshall Field, Clarence Francis, Ray Rubicam, Beardsley Ruml, R. R. Deupree, and Fowler McCormick, all of whom they had considered for the American Policy Commission. For reasons unrecorded, Secretary Jones rejected Luce, Field, Rubicam, and McCormick, as well as Paul Mazur and H. W. Prentiss.

But, as he reached here and there throughout the twelve Federal Reserve Districts, which he used as the basis for the national organization he was now building, Secretary Jones was not attempting to create a personal or political organization. He had not yet announced it as his policy, but from the beginning he had rejected the idea of the committee as a permanent or even official adjunct of the department. Very soon he was to tell the men who had answered his call that they were on their own, except for such advice and technical help as the government could give them.

Nor did Secretary Jones agree with Owen D. Young—whom he first considered for the post of chairman of the group—that the committee should be anything except a businessman's group. He turned a deaf ear to Young's suggestion that it be a tripartite group, with equal representation by business, labor, and agriculture. If labor wished to make its postwar plans, well and good; and if other segments wished to join in, he had no desire to stop them. But always his concept was a huge, national welding of big and small business and industry for the common purpose of averting postwar unemployment and boosting postwar production. On this he was adamant, as he was on most things he believed in.

Secretary Jones's telephone calls brought twelve men, one from each Federal Reserve District, into the first board of trustees of the as yet unnamed organization: from Boston, Ralph E.

Flanders; New York, Owen D. Young; Philadelphia, Thomas B. McCabe; Cleveland, Charles R. Hook; Richmond, John Stewart Bryan; Atlanta, Harrison Jones; Chicago, Paul G. Hoffman; St. Louis, Chester C. Davis; Minneapolis, James Ford Bell; Kansas City, James M. Kemper; Dallas, W. L. Clayton; and San Francisco, Eric A. Johnston.

All through the late winter and early spring of 1942 Secretary Jones, Wayne C. Taylor, Folsom, Hoffman, Benton, and Carroll L. Wilson brought the loose ends together. On June 9, Secretary Jones called a meeting in his office of all concerned, after having sent each, in strictest confidence, an eight-page agenda setting forth the objective and proposed procedures.

In the rather stark words of a Report of Meeting with the Secretary of Commerce that survives, there was general agreement "that the committee is to conduct itself strictly as a business group dedicated to improving the performance of business in carrying out its own organic public duties: namely, the supply of goods to our families and jobs to our citizens. Thus the Committee is to avoid assiduously any tendency towards promoting the special interests of business itself as such. Equally important, it is to refrain from any implication that the Committee seeks to speak for the nation, or even to deal with, the public responsibilities or special interests of other groups in the economy, such as labor, agriculture or Government."

The major aim was to "promote commerce after the war." Its specific tasks were to be the work toward the "full, prompt restoration of our American standard of living; the steady maintenance and continual enhancement of this standard; and the efficient, effective employment *for these purposes* of all persons able and willing to work."

Undersecretary Taylor was empowered to create an organizing committee and he chose R. R. Deupree, Marion B. Folsom, Paul G. Hoffman, Eric A. Johnston, and Thomas B. McCabe, with Arthur Kudner, New York advertising executive, as publicity consultant.

One of the committee's first jobs was to nominate a chairman and working committees for the board of trustees. The group agreed that "the conservative promotion of the Committee's efforts would be jeopardized if the Chairman were a leader of such outstanding national prominence that his very name would attract an exaggerated public attention and perhaps lead to un-warranted expectations." They preferred a "forward-looking, energetic chairman, widely and favorably known to business, but unencumbered with undue national prominence."

This position ran counter to the preference Secretary Jones had expressed for Owen D. Young; but Young had said he was unavailable. In the midst of the organizing committee's discussion, Paul Hoffman had to leave the room to answer an urgent call. When he returned he discovered that he had been nominated by his fellow committeemen. He accepted, with the proviso that his close associate William Benton be named for the vice-chairmanship.

When the committee's choices were relayed to Secretary Jones, they met with his approval. He was especially pleased with the choice of Benton, for he had been somewhat disturbed by the seeming bigness of the enterprises represented. He fore-saw in this respect the grounds on which the group would be attacked in its early years by "liberal" publications. Also, he liked Benton because of his youth (Benton was only forty-one at the time) and he thought of him as a "small businessman" without the stigma of "Wall Street."

A list of potential trustees also was set up and Benton and others took to the road to pull the desired group together. When Benton approached Beardsley Ruml, the first thing the latter did was ask to see a copy of the group's by-laws. When Benton said none existed, Ruml refused to consider participation without them. So Benton, who says he had until then never read a set of by-laws, undertook to write them. They became the center of serious discussion and continuing importance, and Ruml became a trustee.

On July 19, the organizers met in a strained national atmosphere hardly conducive to the creation of an organization dedicated to bettering the postwar world. Most people's minds were on costly defeats on the battlefront and other grim events. The fall of Corregidor was but two months old. Enemy submarines continued to exact a fiery toll off the East coast and in the Caribbean Sea. The Battle of Midway had broken the gloom somewhat, but Rommel the Fox was still stalking unhindered across North Africa and Sebastopol had just been yielded by the Russians. The group wisely decided that this was not the time for public announcement about postwar planning. But they went to work, nonetheless.

Hoffman and Benton were formally elected. They accepted Secretary Jones's offer to release Carroll Wilson from the Commerce Department to act as executive secretary and they named Cyril Scott Fletcher, a brilliant salesman and organizer already loaned by the Studebaker Corporation, to direct the field operations. They set a first annual budget of $250,000 and agreed that it should be raised on a broad basis. In this they adopted the view expressed by Alfred P. Sloan, Jr., in a letter to Clarence Francis:

"Personally, I think it is a mistake to get too large an amount, relatively, from too small a number of people. The reaction is bound to be that there are a few financing the thing for their own selfish purposes. It ought to be a big broad movement on the part of business to attempt, through the scientific approach, to develop a plan which will really be helpful in the way of perpetuating free enterprise after the war is over."

The question of what to call themselves plagued the group. They pored over a list of more than 200 suggestions, including the "Organization for the Public Good," and a wide variety of plays on "the American System," "the American way of life" and other clichés of the world of business. None of the names on the list survived. Some unknown genius, more interested in description than propaganda, suggested "The Committee for Economic Development through Commerce and Industry." The latter phrase was dropped and on September 3, the Committee for Economic Development was incorporated in the District of Columbia.

The next day, at the first official meeting of the trustees of CED, Paul Hoffman read from the certificate of incorporation the rather solemn words which set forth the reason for all the hard work and activity of the past many weeks:

"To foster, promote, conduct, encourage and finance scientific research, education, training and publication in the broad field of economics in order that industry and commerce may be in a position in the postwar period to make their full contribution to high and secure standards of living for people in all walks of life through maximum employment and high productivity in our domestic economy; to promote and carry out these objects, purposes and principles in a free society without regard to and independently of the special interests of any group in the body politic, either political, social or economic."

A long step from the University of Chicago campus had been taken; but there were many steps yet to go.

THREE

"Look Who's Planning!"

ON THE morning of January 2, 1943, the *New York Times* devoted its entire second page to two stories. One was the full text of the New Year's Day rantings of Adolf Hitler. But nearly one-third of the page was occupied by a story on which the headline ran: JOBS FOR 55,000,000 IS POST-WAR PLAN.

The article stressed the belief, or hope, that if American business, regardless of the postwar plans of others, started at once to plan properly, it could be ready at war's close to create 9 million more jobs than there had been in the United States in 1940.

The nation "must produce and sell an annual output between $135 and 150 billion, or 34 to 40 per cent more than in 1940, when the national income was approximately $100 billion," the story said. If this were accomplished, it went on, an approximation of full employment could be achieved. The authority cited was the Committee for Economic Development which, it was announced almost incidentally, had been organized some four months earlier.

For a group of businessmen, able to speak in an official capacity for more than 20-billion dollars' worth of corporate assets* and about to launch a national program designed to affect the lives of millions of people and penetrate the greatest of industrial empires and the smallest of small businesses, the committee had been singularly—and deliberately—reticent.

Although here and there its name had crept into print in connection with "field tests," no publicity had appeared nationally, thanks to careful management under the watchful eye of Arthur Kudner. As more and more local committees were organized, the need for publishing an authoritative announcement had grown, but the organizers were determined not to introduce themselves until they had something of substance to say.

Press reaction to their announcement, which received national attention, was mixed. Conservative, business-minded publications, such as *Time, Newsweek,* and *Business Week,* were impressed, perhaps as much by the corporations represented by the CED trustees as by the optimistic forecasts and the proposed program itself. On the other hand these same names, smacking of big business and monopoly, caused the liberal press to view the new organization with skeptical alarm. If to *Business Week* the CED trustees were "predominantly on the liberal side in political and economic thinking in business," they were not recognizable in these terms to the *New Republic* or *The Nation.*

"Look who's planning!" the former was soon to scoff in a rather bitter article written by Helen Fuller, in which she sought to link CED closely to the National Association of Manufacturers—and even to "America First." In the creation of the new committee Miss Fuller saw a revival of the old NAM-inspired National Industrial Conference Board, and she asserted that the

* This is approximately the worth of the corporations represented by the original small board of trustees. In 1959, 59 trustees were chairmen, presidents, or top executives of industrial corporations with assets (according to *Fortune,* July 1959) of $59,938,998,000. The corporations represented by 32 of these 59 trustees were among the 100 largest industrial corporations in the U.S., with total assets of $49,062,278,000. These do not include commercial banks, merchandising firms, life insurance companies, or public utility systems represented on the board of trustees, by then grown to approximately 200 members.

"kind of plant-by-plant planning for full production and full employment the CED is inspiring is as truly isolationist in character as was the America First movement." She ominously warned: "If the United Nations are to be an actuality, the Committee for Economic Development's approach to post-war planning cannot be allowed to prevail."

It was not really surprising that there should have been many others who wondered with Miss Fuller if the new committee was what it pretended to be. To the general public, at least, its board of trustees, with few exceptions, was not widely known. Many of the businessmen active in the field-development operations, on the other hand, were known as ultraconservatives. If one leafed through the list of regional directors and sought to unravel what appeared to be an interlocking of corporate interests, in which large industries and public utilities seemed to predominate, then there was some reason to suspect the economic and political purity of the untried committee.

The lingering atmosphere of the times was such that this questioning approach was not surprising. In some ways it was salutary. It was not allowed to go unnoticed or unchallenged at CED trustee meetings. Indeed, it was just such articles as Miss Fuller's that led, a few months later, to the publication of CED's *Articles of Faith*, a brilliant dissertation on business liberalism and a concise setting forth of CED's major aims and purposes written by William Benton, which has taken a historic place in the literature of what has sometimes been called the New Conservatism.

In many minds the unsavory role which some businessmen had played in the rise of fascism and Hitlerism was not forgotten. The fierce labor struggles of the 1930's, when the words and acts of many business leaders had seemingly given the lie to the phrase "It can't happen here," had left their ideological scars. Bigness, too, was still a curse in many American minds. And the "strike of capital" had not endeared all industrialists to the people. For a businessman's committee to be talking about full employment was an anomalous situation. Under these circumstances it was difficult for many to read patriotism into the postwar planning ideas sponsored by representatives of, say, the American Rolling Mills.

Liberals also were shocked when, just one week after CED had announced its creation, Congress peevishly did away with the National Resources Planning Board, one of the last surviving children of Dr. New Deal. In spite of the many attacks upon this governmental bureau, there were some unbiased observers who considered it a valuable adjunct of the government which served a most useful purpose. Its contributions to postwar planning had been intelligently carried out and several of its recent reports had gone a long way to remove the taint of its more leftish and ambitious early efforts. Now Congress demolished it and forbade any other agency to assume its functions. This action led some to ask, with the *New Republic*, whether Congress was "turning over the direction of postwar planning for American security and well-being to American business"—a horrible thought for all New Dealers.

The close association of CED with the Department of Commerce, and especially with Jesse Jones, confused many into believing that CED was at least a quasi-governmental organization. Its identification by its initials added to the confusion on the part of liberals and conservatives alike. The public therefore was not entirely to blame for suspecting that the government, or at least the Secretary of Commerce, was trying, through the creation of CED, to evade its own tremendous responsibilities for preventing postwar inflation and unemployment and thus taking early measures to avoid the general economic collapse which, if history was to be believed, would be the inevitable aftermath of war.

Nor was all the skepticism on the liberal side. One New York businessman expressed in a letter to Paul Hoffman the viewpoint of conservative critics when he commented upon a speech the CED chairman had made in which he had stated that business could and should employ 56,000,000 persons in the immediate postwar period.

"You are making an implied promise that is impossible of fulfillment," the critic wrote. "The public and the lawmakers must realize that industry alone cannot and should not be expected to bear the brunt of guaranteeing full employment in the postwar years, or at any other time. . . . With all the good will in the world it is utterly impossible for the thousands of individual concerns in this country to assume any collective responsibility or indeed to more than try to do their best under the pressure of natural forces, including the age-old law of supply and demand."

On the whole, however, the introduction of CED was well received and even recognized in many quarters as revolutionary. The daring imagination of its program, based as it was on the theory that full employment was a necessary condition to prosperity, had an instant appeal to the average American, especially coming as it did from the side of business rather than of labor. It is interesting to note that organized labor accepted the appearance of CED without any antagonistic comment that has survived.

The fact that CED refrained from attempting to make a big splash in the press may have had much to do with its calm acceptance. In addition, the officers of CED had sought from the beginning to create a friendly climate of opinion. In the still prevalent atmosphere of business-government antagonism, the need to approach the Roosevelt administration in an amicable spirit was appreciated. During his conscientious search for talent for the Research Division, William Benton talked with scores of persons, among them Secretary of State Cordell Hull, Secretary of War Frank Knox, and old New Dealers such as Thurman Arnold, the trust buster, and Milo Perkins. Other officials of the State, Treasury, and Agriculture Departments as well as the Federal Reserve Board were kept informed.

Since the organization was not working either for or against any specific legislation, its tax-exempt status did not inhibit the presentation of its aims and purposes to members of Congress at dinners given by Hoffman and others. In similar fashion it got its story across to executives of the American Federation of Labor and the then Committee of Industrial Organizations, whose participation was not invited but whose understanding was considered essential to success.

The program about to be launched by the new organization was divided into two parts: the Field Development Division and the Research Division. Even more than was recognized by its sponsors, the two-part program was closely interwoven. The research that was contemplated, although practical in conception and pragmatic in purpose, lent to the CED idea a quality of scientific and intellectual adventure that was unique among existing business organizations.

In academic circles there was much speculation as to what results might come from the facts and figures being assembled by its small professional staff and the businessmen who were taking an active part in the process. Ralph Flanders, chairman of the Research Division, was already known as a curious-minded individual whose own inquiries into the problem of unemployment in the thirties had not gone unnoticed. Now, working closely with him, was Dr. Theodore O. Yntema, a member of the University of Chicago faculty, who was described at the time as a "moderately conservative economist of top professional standing who can talk business English," and whose presence offset the somewhat startling (to some) appearance of Gardiner Means, who was brought into CED when the National Resources Planning Board was so summarily done away with.

It has been said, not without some justification, that the hiring of Means cost CED $100,000. While the figure may have been exaggerated, several conservative businessmen drew away their financial support because of his presence on the staff. The founders of CED never questioned his professional status as an economist, and the complaints that recurred sporadically over the years were regarded as a price worth paying for academic freedom. Gardiner Means remained with CED until his retirement in 1958.

While Flanders and his fellow members of the Research Committee were launching their investigations in three major categories—the attainment of high employment, the maintenance of a high level of production, and solutions to the sequels of war policies such as price controls, rationing, war-plant disposal, termination of contracts, and surplus war inventories—the more volatile Field Development Division was preparing its assault upon the indifference and ignorance of the American businessman.

The first task was search for talent. Paul Hoffman did not have to go outside the Studebaker Corporation to find the man who was quickly to prove himself the ideal choice to take command of the national campaign, under the over-all direction of Marion B. Folsom, chairman of the Field Development Division. If Yntema could "talk business English," Cyril Scott Fletcher breathed it.

Like Hoffman, his mentor, "Scotty" Fletcher was a born salesman. This Australian-born son of the founder of Kings College at the University of Queensland quite probably would have followed the family tradition and become a teacher if he had not taken a summer job with the Sydney distributor of Studebaker cars during his last year in preparatory school. After graduation he became the distributor's advertising manager, moved on to head the used-car division, ending up as special manufacturer's representative covering all Australia. He was called to South Bend, Indiana, headquarters of Studebaker, and after much sales experience in this country and overseas became sales director of the corporation.

When Hoffman sought to beat the depression in the automobile industry by introducing the famous Studebaker Champion, Fletcher headed the sales force which raised Studebaker from behind Ford, Chrysler, and Hudson, as the fourth largest independent automobile manufacturer, to the largest of the non-

General Motors enterprises. He was a natural organizer as well as salesman, and Hoffman had turned to him to head the fund-raising campaign for United China Relief when he took over the chairmanship of that organization. When this job ended, with nine million dollars raised, Hoffman called him to CED.

In his new job Fletcher quickly found that a great many more men than Arthur Upgren had discovered were now seriously concerned with postwar planning. Not only was Prince of General Electric devoting time and attention to the future, but such men as T. M. MacGowan of Firestone Rubber and Tire, Elihu Hedges of Eastman Kodak, and Bert White of the Liberty National Bank of Buffalo, to name only a few, were similarly engaged. Bert White was already deep in the preparation of a program for community action by the industrialists and businessmen of his area.

The machinery Fletcher had to work with was both simple and complex. At the top of the pyramidical structure was the Field Development Division's chairman, Marion B. Folsom. His primary duty was to carry out the injunction of the by-laws to "stimulate planning on the part of business enterprises for their own future after the war and to develop material for the furtherance of such planning." Working with Folsom and Fletcher was a staff of about fifteen persons which, from time to time, was augmented by volunteers so that almost always there were between thirty and forty persons actively on the working roster. Many of them were business executives on leave from their companies, newspapermen, and economists and analysts from the staffs of various concerns. Some contributed their services for nothing to take on special tasks. Others, on full-time leave, worked full time, usually at a sacrifice in salary.

Nearly 3,000 community CED's, located in every state of the Union, were established during the war years.* They operated under regional committees strategically located in each of the

* By actual count, 2,947.

Federal Reserve districts. The twelve regional chairmen were not trustees but were appointed by them. They were, in fact as well as theory, the voice of CED in the sections under their direction. They chose the district or state chairmen for each area of 100,000 population within their regions. They set up their own committees, without much if any direction from national headquarters. Proposals for the national field program came from them and they, in turn, administered the national program in their districts, working downward through their own committees. They could advise the trustees, but they had no vote in national policies.

This structure was not as cumbersome as it might seem. In each instance the regional chairman was a businessman of state- or district-wide prominence, president or board chairman of an important industrial or commercial firm or corporation, known in his region for business leadership. Few were mere figureheads; some, like Walter D. Fuller, president of the Curtis Publishing Company, Philadelphia, or Harry W. Zinsmaster, president of the Zinsmaster Bread Company of Duluth, Minnesota, or Dr. William McClellan, chairman, Union Electric Company, St. Louis, took their responsibilities seriously and devoted long and effortful hours to CED.

But it was the local or community committee which was the real heart of the CED postwar planning program. At first the local committees were restricted to areas of 10,000 population, but soon any community anywhere, no matter what its size or industrial importance, was allowed to set up its own CED. Many of these sprang into being on their own initiative without any prodding from the national organization. All were actually independent units, allowed to do things in their own way and at their own expense. Their cooperation with the parent organization was wholly voluntary, as far as their own community was concerned. Local operations were not dictated by CED's New York office. But the national body sent them material, offered them advice, helped them in any way possible, furnishing them with direction, and sending representatives when requested to show them how others had solved the problems facing them. The national committee had a national responsibility, however, and, while it set no rigid rules and regulations for the local committees, it never allowed itself to forget the national economic forest for the local trees.

The typical community CED was organized for broad community participation. Its chairman was usually the best-known businessman in the district. Working with him was the regional manager, also a volunteer. All except the very smallest local CED's engaged a full-time executive secretary. As a rule, and by the national CED's request, he was, wherever possible, the secretary of the local Chamber of Commerce. A number of vice-chairmen, usually chosen from among younger businessmen of the community, also were on the committee. If the community were large enough, the local CED set up various local "action divisions" made up of active members of industry, commerce, labor, and agriculture. Chairmen of these divisions formed the executive committee. These chairmen worked closely with industrial executives, merchants, tradesmen, farmers, and often with local labor organizations.

If the community called for it, the local CED's organized committees on the special problems of small business, fact-finding and local research committees, education committees, library committees, and fraternal and service organization committees, all of whom worked together to study and report on the economic problems peculiar to their own localities. And often the community CED's created, or worked with, established local advisory committees composed of civic leaders, municipal officers, teachers, churchmen, and other nonbusiness people, who might be expected to help in the larger community problems not entirely removed from the postwar economic problems that were CED's major concern.

The trustees were forever emphasizing to the staff the never-to-be-forgotten dictum that CED was not trying to impose a national plan upon the economy, and that the small entrepreneur was even more important in the over-all picture than the huge enterprises. Although some of the best brains of Wall Street, Washington, and Madison Avenue were gathered together in CED, there was a great concern not to force tricks and gadgets upon the local CED's. What the national group produced was designed to nourish the grass roots. The tending of them was left as much as possible to those who knew the home pastures best. A continuous and voluminous exchange of information and ideas, based upon experience, thus flowed back and forth between Main Street and Madison Avenue.

In order to facilitate this two-way flow the Field Development Division established early in 1943 a monthly news organ, *CED News*, edited by Kay Smallzried. It presented a running account of activities in all the twelve regional areas and was the repository of official CED policies as set by the trustees. In spite of the paper shortage, it achieved a circulation of 60,000 copies eventually. Also to aid in the dissemination of CED information, an Information Division was created in 1943, with Anthony Hyde as director.

Such was the basic CED field organization, but there were other important CED divisions which rounded out the national functions of the committee. One, known collectively as the Action and Advisory Committees, was in three parts: manufacturing, marketing, and new materials, processes, and designs. All told there were twenty-seven such committees, closely allied with CED activities. These brought together the postwar planning work of all the national trade and professional associations. At first their work was coordinated by CED under an Industrial Advisory Board, later known as the National Advisory Committee, which included, as well as the chairmen of each action group, representatives from the National Foreign Trade Council, the National Association of Purchasing Agents, the National Association of Credit Men, the American Management Association, and the United States Chamber of Commerce.

These groups together did some of the most effective work in preparing handbooks for the practical assistance of manufacturers and businessmen, and they helped spread planning information to the 3,000 CED local groups. By July, 1945, some 250,000 members of local trade association groups were receiving CED material through this setup. As we shall see, one of the most dramatic of CED efforts was the work of one of these action groups.

Another important committee came into the CED organization before the end of the first year. One of the most widespread criticisms of CED, as we have seen, was that it was too greatly concerned with Big Business. Paul Hoffman was especially sensitive to this accusation, which was not too accurate, in any case. This charge was met by establishing a Committee on the Special Problems of Small Business. From the beginning the Research Division had been concerned with this aspect of the economics of the country, but the long process of research was not geared to bring the committee's thoughts on the subject before the public at this early date. Its first report was not to be ready until February, 1944. In *Jobs, Key to the Maintenance of Prosperity*, Hoffman reiterated the consensus of the trustees when he said: "The Committee is not overly concerned with the larger corporations. They can take care of themselves. . . . It is the smaller businesses—tens of thousands of them all over the country —which are going to need encouragement and help in getting their programs under way. . . . In the aggregate, the small businessman provides many millions with their livelihood. They are the grassroots from which our business economy grows. . . ."

In the fall of 1942 CED, setting out to explore the potentialities of the grass-roots regions, chose three cities which, preliminary investigation showed, provided problems typical of those the committee would face in attempting to reach its goal of establishing a CED committee in all of the more than 1,000 communities with 10,000 or more population. These were Peoria, Illinois, Wheeling, West Virginia, and Reading, Pennsylvania.

The "Peoria Story," as it was called in the press, made CED history. Peoria was selected because this city of 122,000 persons, with about 6,000 of them in the Armed Forces, was considered to be a representative Midwest manufacturing town. Its adjustment to war production had been fairly simple, for most of its factories continued during the war to make the same products they had before; although some plants (such as Altorfer Brothers Company, a manufacturer of washing machines) had fairly serious conversion jobs to accomplish and would be faced with similarly serious reconversion problems. For most plants, however, the jobs of conversion and of reconversion looked easy and seemed to be in miniature the same problems that were facing the entire country.

In November Ralph Budd, president of the Burlington Railroad and CED's regional chairman for the 7th Federal Reserve district, met with twenty business and industrial executives and presented them with the CED plan. Reasonably impressed, the Peoria group chose Walter Gardner, general sales manager of Keystone Steel and Wire Company, as local CED chairman.

Gardner moved quickly and within a few days had named a six-man executive committee, set up an action committee headed by Frank L. Ross of Willamette Hyster Company, a research committee under the leadership of G. R. Roelfs of Central Illinois Light Company, and a public relations committee under Theodore Fleming of Fleming Potter Company. Roelf's committee surveyed the industrial situation, discovered that there were forty-nine manufacturing concerns each employing fifty or more people. Of these only four employed more than 1,000 workers.

By mid-December representatives of all the forty-nine companies met. They were asked to assign to some group or individual within their firms the authority to prepare a report on postwar planning, to investigate possibilities for new products, improvements, materials, markets, and opportunities and, most important, to fill out a check sheet. It was from the answers to this check sheet that CED expected to accumulate the data from which could be drawn a picture of the postwar economic potential of the entire United States.

This asked just three questions: what was the company's employment in 1940; its employment at the present time; and its estimated postwar employment. Honest answers were asked for, and nothing else. To get these answers the company usually had to appoint an executive to analyze the business and its plans. At the same time the local research committee was digging out other facts and statistics on the various factors which would affect the community in the postwar world: community liquidity, farm income, deferred demand for products, and potential employment outside of industry. Some research committees even went so far as to write to servicemen to find out if they planned to return to their home towns to work after the war. The community government, too, was asked to prepare memoranda on possible future civic improvements so that the number of jobs available from local public works might be estimated.

The short questionnaire had met with some opposition when being prepared on the grounds that it was "too subjective" and therefore "unscientific." But it appealed to businessmen because of its brevity and simplicity. It served two purposes: to bring forth facts and, at the same time, to stimulate action. In 1944 the Bureau of Labor Statistics tested the check sheets for accuracy in forty communities and found them surprisingly accurate. The Bureau reported the CED technique of determining the postwar employment potential to be "as fine a method as has been developed to 'get the facts and to stimulate postwar planning in the communities.' "

When Gardner's committeemen began circulating the questionnaire in Peoria they found—as did others in other communities later—that the vast majority of employers had given little if any thought to the problems they would face in transition from war to peace. But when faced with the problem of what would happen when war orders suddenly stopped coming in and unemployment hit the country—and Peoria—they began to think. Many at first felt that the "inevitable postwar depression" would be a problem which only the federal government could solve. But, when faced with the CED sales talk that this was essentially a problem for private enterprise, of which they were a part, however small, they took the question seriously. The majority of the employers approached, enjoying a new prosperity born of war contracts, wanted to keep on making money. They accepted the sheets, did the work involved in filling them out, and began looking ahead to making new products, or finding new markets, or new methods of sales and distribution—when peace came.

From the returns of the check sheets distributed in Peoria the action committee was able to report early in 1943 to CED national headquarters on the results of this first nongovernmental postwar survey and estimate of potential employment.

Of the forty-nine companies approached, all but four reported. These forty-five companies employed 97.5 per cent of the workers in Peoria plants. In 1942 practically all these plants were engaged 100 per cent in war production. The survey indicated a total employment of 30,000 at the time. The prediction of postwar employment was 29,000. In 1940, however, only 22,000 Peorians had been employed by these same firms.

A further conclusion of the action committee was that, if employment was maintained at this rate in factories, it could also be maintained at a similarly high rate in retail, wholesale, and service establishments. Although such organizations were not included in the first survey, a later check of employers of some 2,500 persons in service occupations revealed that they thought they could hold employment, under such circumstances, at 1942's top figure.

The Peoria test (and the simultaneous tests at Wheeling and Reading) persuaded the CED trustees and staff that the CED idea was sound, that American industry and business *could* plan a future that would circumvent the postwar let-down. Of perhaps more importance, however, was the dismaying discovery that postwar planning was not under way in most companies and that it would get started only if adequate stimulation was applied by such an organization as CED.

This, of course, meant continued work, for it was only on a second or third call by the committeemen that apathetic employers were stirred to action. The need for a national organization was apparent: handbooks, manuals, and reports that only such a group could supply were essential to guide the local committees and employers in an orderly and somewhat scientific approach to the work and study necessary to plan intelligently for the future.

The great achievement of the Peoria test lay not so much in the figures, which were only estimates (and were revised several times before the end of the war) as in the eventual willingness, as Ralph Budd put it, of management when prodded "to squeeze hours out of war-time work to set up individual plans for translating victory into jobs and preparing for peacetime opportunities."

Although the Peoria test was "typical" there was no set pattern of local committee development. In Reading, Pennsylvania, the local Chamber of Commerce had already commenced postwar planning, and the local CED committee was organized around this nucleus. In Wheeling, West Virginia, local employers themselves set up CED committees to cooperate with existing local organizations. In Baltimore the Mayor's Committee on Post War Planning became the local CED. In the Philadelphia region Walter Fuller stressed local autonomy in selecting district chairmen, asking leading businessmen to name one who held the respect and confidence of all the community, thus assuring that local leaders would support the man chosen. In all communities the local committees tried to maintain close cooperation with Rotary, Kiwanis, and Lions clubs as a matter of good public relations. In Peoria and elsewhere the hardest task was not to get chairmen but to stir the communities into action and to maintain interest.

When, as in the first count in Peoria, the estimated future jobs fell below the estimated labor demand, the committeemen would go back to the industries, commercial firms, and farmers armed with material produced by the national trade associations and other divisions of CED. These were often highly technical, but they were understandable treatises on planning for new production, new products, expanded plant facilities, better and different services, new sales methods, new products, more economical operations, and better personnel management. The tracts would be implemented often by clinics and forums on the special problems of individual businesses. The work of experts in various lines, these manuals bored deep into business techniques, were detailed in their suggestions and methods, and afforded many executives what amounted to postgraduate courses in their own fields. They were competent documents and not just exhortations of press agents. In Paul Hoffman's words these presentations "distilled the plethora of know-how about postwar planning for individual enterprises."

Even before the Peoria test had got under way in the autumn of 1942, the founders of CED had asked the Department of Commerce for estimates on the level of employment and gross product that would supply a satisfactory postwar economy, one in which, as Paul Hoffman put it, "neither mass unemployment nor mass governmental employment" would play a part. The answer the Department came up with was that about 56 million employed and a gross product in the neighborhood of 142 billion dollars (in 1940 prices) would be the goal to aim at. In other words, from 7 to 10 million more jobs and an expansion in productivity of from 30–45 per cent over 1940 (the peak prewar year) were needed to reach this goal. It was on this projection that CED based its aims and philosophy as it set out on its self-appointed task.

FOUR

Markets and Jobs for All

THE YEAR 1944 was a year of great decision, a year of quickened hope and approaching victory, and a year of vast confusions. It was, too, a year of omens and portents. It swung, as the historian Bruce Catton has put it, like a gate to the future.

The year 1944 was the year in which the Allies, under General Eisenhower, crossed the Channel and invaded the continent of Europe, and the year in which the American forces, under General MacArthur, began in earnest to avenge the retreat from Bataan. In September the guns of the First Army lofted their shells for the first time into the Nazis' homeland. In October the American forces seized the eastern coast of Leyte Island in the Philippines. The next month saw Russian troops sweep across the border of Slovakia. And, in cold December, the Nazis launched their last-ditch offensive, that which was to be called the Battle of the Bulge.

This was the year which was to see Franklin Delano Roosevelt elected President for the fourth time and a man little known beyond Capitol Hill, Harry S. Truman, elected Vice President. This was the year that saw the still bitter and lonely Al Smith die, forgotten in the midst of the presidential campaign, and the year that saw Wendell Willkie, his *One World* still a best seller, die suddenly without having given his blessing to the ambitious Governor of New York, who was vainly seeking to oust the tiring Commander-in-Chief from his command.

This was the year of hope—of Bretton Woods and Dumbarton Oaks, symbols of the future and the peace that was to make the world so different from any world yet known. It was also the year that saw the first cutbacks, the first slackening in production, and the first labor layoffs since the arsenal of democracy had got going full blast.

In Washington in those days of confusion and accomplishment —for, in spite of all the struggle, things *did* move—there were many in high places who looked askance on all this talk about the postwar world. The military men, whose power was as great as their mistrust of civilian leadership, were convinced that official and unofficial concentration on postwar planning was, to say the least, interfering with the progress of war.

But in spite of their feelings many things happened and kept happening to direct the attention of the American people to the postwar world. The invasion of Italy in the autumn of 1943, the satisfactory progress of the war in Russia, and an increasing awareness that the invasion of Europe (which, everyone knew, must be a success) was soon to happen—all this aroused an increasing interest in the problem of what would come about when peace arrived. It was not only a few businessmen in CED who wanted to prepare and plan for that day. The people wanted it, too.

Congress, too, was not neglecting the hoped-for and prayed-for future, when war would end. In November, 1943, Senator Walter F. George took the chairmanship of the newly created Special Committee on Postwar Economic Policy and Planning— a title that smacked of the old New Deal which President Roosevelt, in his forthcoming 1944 budget message, was to intimate would be reborn after Hitler and Tojo were defeated. In the House, Representative William M. Colmer, a Mississippi Democrat, headed a similar committee. Marion B. Folsom was director of this committee's staff. While the guns still roared across two oceans and men still died, Senator George's committee held public hearings on such matters as the cancellation of war contracts, the disposition of surplus property, and industrial demobilization and reconversion.

Planning for the orderly transition from war to peace was a fetish with Donald Nelson, the rather aloof but effective civilian head of the War Production Board. But the military leaders scorned his ideas, infiltrated his department, and opened a barrage which, many thought, was an outright assault on the patriotism of the people on the home front. It may have been all right for the Commander-in-Chief to say that "demobilization begins before hostilities cease," to talk of attaining "a permanently high level of income and a correspondingly high standard of living," and to propose, as the major aim of reconversion policy, the "stimulation of private investment and employment," and even, a few days later, to suggest legislation leading to a postwar federal highway program, in cooperation with the states, that would provide 35,000 miles of new highways. But to the military this smacked of something close to subversion.

The fact was that the war emergency had piled up so many unfilled needs on the economy that any thinking person knew that the process of reconversion would have to begin far in advance of the actual end of the war. Yet there was some strength to the military's argument. After all, the invasion of Europe had not begun; and too much talk of peace, of lessening controls even where manpower, manufacturing facilities, and materials were available to produce needed civilian goods, could be dangerous. It might well be true that the Armed Forces had oversupplied themselves, that the American worker had done an amazing and loyal job, and that, if there were any lack of supplies for the fighting man, it was transportation and not production that was to blame. But it was better not to say so. People might become complacent.

In St. Louis three Army officers made speeches damning postwar planning in general and CED in particular. At this same time, the plea came to CED from some Midwestern community chairmen urging the committee to "soft-pedal" its postwar planning during "this critical phase of the war." But Chairman Hoffman rejected this plea. The winning of the war, he stressed, *was* of paramount importance (and he never failed to stress this in his many speeches) but the winning of the peace was not to be neglected.

The Committee for Economic Development did not become publicly embroiled in the argument between the military and the civilian. Instead, it concentrated upon its dedicated task of creating a plant-by-plant, city-by-city, and industry-by-industry device whereby, when the time came, the producers on whom a stable economy depended might prevent the chaos that could work havoc with the national well-being.

The campaign to reach as many as possible of the estimated 2 million business employers in the nation proceeded at full speed. Detailed plans were drawn up to encourage them and help them be ready "with bold, intelligent plans for expansion at the end of the war." At the same time the research committee was proceeding with its examination of national policies of government, business, agriculture, and labor "which will seriously affect the levels of production and employment after the war."

At the end of the first full year, CED had created 822 local committees; by the end of 1944 this had increased to slightly more than 2,000 community CED's, with more than 50,000 businessmen participating. It was estimated that almost every town in the United States with 10,000 or more population had a functioning CED committee.

The talents available to various national professional associations were also mobilized to serve these local units. The Association of Consulting Engineers, for example, prepared three handbooks designed as scientific guides for planning for executives in manufacturing, wholesale, and retail fields. By the end of 1944 more than 400,000 copies had been printed and distributed.

The National Society of Sales Executives prepared a set of five handbooks on the selection and training of sales personnel. This group and the National Federation of Sales Executives used them as the basis for "sales clinics" throughout the country in which sales representatives from more than 10,000 companies participated.

The American Bankers Association distributed a handbook on the postwar credit problems of businessmen to more than 15,000 banks. There were even handbooks and slide films prepared for use in rural towns and villages too small to be reached by regular local committees. And these were distributed with the cooperation of farm publications and the Western Newspaper Union.

Here, of course, was more than the beginning of what might well develop into a powerful national organization. There were fears in some quarters that this might happen. To forestall this the trustees emphasized their belief that, although success in the postwar battle against unemployment could be obtained only by active participation of the majority of business leaders, such participation "could never be obtained by methods of remote control, or by the application of some 'national plan.' " Thus the stress on the local autonomy of the committees continued.

But even as the movement for postwar planning grew, so did criticism for engaging in it.

"This is going to be an easy peace to lose," Paul Hoffman warned the National Association of Manufacturers in answer to the criticism that mounted to new heights with the Battle of the Bulge still in doubt. "Careful preparation at this time is essential."

Although he admitted that "undue publicity on postwar planning should be avoided until the present crisis is over" and stressed that "the war comes first," he did not deviate from the conviction that "we have this educational job to do."

"What I don't want to see is a retreat," he said. "If false thinking should slow down postwar planning, and 5,000,000 people should be thrown out of work on V-E Day, then it would be a job to win the *second* phase of the war."

There were complaints in business circles, voiced even by some of CED's trustees, about being too specific in enunciating postwar employment aims in figures. The *National City Bank Bulletin* for December, 1944, for example, objected to the use of figures in setting up a postwar goal for employment or production. But CED never abandoned its expressed assumption that there should and could be 8 or 10 million more jobs and a 35–45 per cent increase in production, in the first full year of peace, than there had been in 1940.

Fears also were expressed at what was termed the "loose use of the term full employment." Research Director Yntema remarked that "CED does not decide upon the terminology of the people," and added that "what we should do is try to explain what is meant by 'full employment.' " And Paul Hoffman provided a succinct and typical answer.

"When 'full employment' is used by the man in the street," he said, "it is used in the same sense as when used by the politician— a job for everyone who wants one. You avoid trouble if you state a goal and put a number on it. . . . To my mind there is nothing quite as dangerous as not having a goal. . . . I want to reiterate, *CED has established goals.*"

As the debate and the planning continued, the new year dawned. If 1944 had been the year of promise, 1945 was destined to be the year of fulfillment. On January 20, in the simplest inaugural ceremony in history, Franklin D. Roosevelt, not yet quite sixty-three years old, stood bareheaded in the zero temperature of a raw winter day and took the oath of office for the fourth time.

On April 12 the world was shocked by his sudden death. It seemed to millions that an era had come to an end. But, although there was time for mourning, there was little time for anything else than carrying on the war. A little man, the compromise of politics, so they said, stepped in with quiet resolution. None knew it then, but with his coming a new, and frightening, era had begun.

In his brief fourth inaugural address President Roosevelt had said, "The trend of civilization is forever upward." On April 25 President Truman, from his desk in Washington, addressed the opening session of the San Francisco Conference with uncertain voice but measured words. Five days later, unbeknownst to the world, Adolf Hitler ended his own life in a bunker in Berlin. Less than two months after FDR had penned his final words— "The only limit to our realization of tomorrow will be our doubts of today. Let us move forward with strong and active faith"—the war in Europe came to an end.

On June 25 fifty nations signed the Charter of Security at San Francisco. Soon Harry Truman and Clement Atlee were putting their heads together with Stalin at Potsdam to determine the future of Germany. At 5:50 on a July morning, a flash that few who saw it fully understood devastated a New Mexican dawn. Less than a month later two similar flashes sent mushrooming clouds above Hiroshima and Nagasaki. At midnight on August 14, Prime Minister Atlee and President Truman announced the surrender of Japan.

Thus quickly, inexorably, the great, victorious, and tragic events moved through the first eight months of 1945, and suddenly that "postwar world," so long talked about and so expectantly anticipated, was at hand.

On August 12, two days before V-J Day, a chorus of dire warning began to be heard throughout the country. From Washington one newspaperman, fresh from visiting various government agencies whose experts might be expected to give an accurate picture of the situation, forecast that V-J Day would see 10 million persons thrown out of jobs, not to mention the millions of veterans who would return to a workless land. His doleful report quoted CIO officials as predicting 10 million unemployed within thirty days of Japan's surrender and said that the experts at the War Production Board counted between 7 and 9 million jobless within ninety days, while at the Labor Department the worst guess was that between 7 and 8 million would be thrown off the national production line before the end of 1945.

Day by day the chorus of despair grew louder. The *New York Times* reported cautiously that "the best government and private estimates" indicated a figure of about 8,000,000 unemployed by the spring of 1946, after which date it was expected to decline. The *Wall Street Journal*, after a grim talk with War Manpower Commission officials, saw no fewer than 6,200,000 jobless by the end of the year. And Robert Nathan, the brilliant economist who was then Deputy Reconversion Director, warned of 8 million idle men and women by the same date. "There are a lot of changes we've got to make in our economic thinking to prevent a depression," Nathan said a short time later. "If nothing is done to stabilize the economy at high levels and to get full employment in another two or three years, then we're going to have a depression that will shake the free enterprise system to its very foundation."

Just five days after V-J Day the front pages of the newspapers and the voices of radio newscasters injected a note of calm reason into this chorus of despair. While Congress, state legislatures, and city officials vied with each other in announcing plans—all well intentioned, some well thought out—to cope with the changed situation, the Committee for Economic Development released the report of its Marketing Committee which dramatically projected and clarified the postwar employment production figures CED had been using.

Optimistically entitled *American Industry Looks Ahead*, the 63-page pamphlet was the joint effort of fifty leading market specialists, 1,406 individual manufacturers, and 158 trade associations, who had worked for eighteen months to take a hard look at the postwar capacities of the nation's twenty leading industries. Although admitting that its conclusions rested on little more than guesswork, it concluded that "if the level of manufacturing volume foreseen by American manufacturing industry materializes, we shall have substantially full employment" in the first full postwar year after reconversion. Since the committee concluded that the war would end within a short time of the report's publication, it assumed this first year would be 1947.

American Industry Looks Ahead assumed that there would actually be three major postwar periods. The first, the transitional period (when industry would reconvert its productive facilities from war to peacetime production) was already at hand when the report appeared. The "transitional unemployment" which was already causing some rather "hysterical comment," it pointed out, should not be allowed to "frighten the public," as obviously it was only temporary.

The second, or intermediary, period would come when industry tried to catch up with the accumulated demands for goods made scarce or unobtainable during the war.

The final period would come with the "shift to a self-sustaining basis," at which time "jobs will depend upon current demand and current income."

While the report "agreed with many economists" that the third period was "basically the one fraught with the greatest danger to our economy and its institutions," *American Industry Looks Ahead* dealt almost entirely with the second period because "its dangers and problems are nearer at hand."

The report alluded to the New Deal goal of 60,000,000 jobs— a phrase made famous by Henry Agard Wallace,* who now sat uneasily in the chair so precipitately abandoned, at F.D.R.'s request, by Jesse Jones—and estimated that this would indeed be the prospective labor force in the first full postwar year. But because about 3,500,000 men would still be in the Armed Forces and because at least 2,500,000 others would make up the inevitable "labor float," the report predicted that only 54,000,000 workers would be needed to approach full employment.

The 1944 labor force, including those in the armed services, was actually 64,000,000 compared to 48,000,000 in 1929, and

* *Sixty Million Jobs*, 1945.

54,100,000 in 1939, when 8,000,000, or 16 per cent, of the nation's potential workers were still without jobs. But, in the first postwar year, the CED report asserted, there would be only 552,000 unemployed, while the number of employed *civilians* would reach the gratifying total of 53,448,000, and might even rise as high as 57,000,000.

The process by which the committee reached this conclusion was simple. It began by asking individual companies to estimate, on their own assumptions, what the probable output of their companies would be in the first full postwar year after a substantial element of industrial reconversion had taken place. After each manufacturer had made his forecast of expected volume, the committee's analysts averaged the forecasts for each of the twenty industries and then totaled the averages to obtain a composite forecast for manufacturing as a whole.

On the basis of this figuring the committee concluded that in physical volume the total manufacturing output for the first full postwar year after reconversion would be 42 per cent greater than in 1939. From this figure it moved to the employment field. Assuming that substantially full employment required 54,000,000 jobs, it calculated that the 42 per cent increase of manufacturing volume over 1939 corresponded to an employment level of 53,500,000 (in round figures), a mere half-million less than full employment.

This optimistic conclusion was built up in two major steps. First, employment in manufacturing was estimated on the basis of assumptions as to weekly wages and average output per man-hour. Second, *total* employment was deduced from manufacturing employment by using a probable ratio based on historical relationships. By means of this chain of assumptions, the probable employment of 53,500,000 and probable unemployment of 3,000,000 was forecast.

The committee said that it was possible to project the *prewar* relationship between manufacturing employment and total employment by mathematical methods which would "strongly suggest" that a figure of 25 per cent or even a little higher might be reached, especially when it was realized that the first full postwar year after reconversion would be a year of "filling accumulated demand for manufactured goods." The committee assumed that manufacturing in 1947 would account for 25.2 per cent of the total civilian employment.

On this basis it calculated that if 13,469,000 persons (exclusive of self-employed) were employed in manufacturing, then the total number of employed civilians should be 53,448,000. After some hedging and pointing out that a change of only 0.5 per cent in the ratio would produce a plus or minus change of about 1,000,000 persons in civilian employment, the report made these conclusions:

"Starting with business's own estimate of manufactures in 1947 ($80,515,000 at 1939 prices), our best (and very rough) guess as to the attendant level of civilian employment is around 53.5 million. Actually civilian employment anywhere between fifty-one and fifty-seven million would be entirely possible and reasonable if the value of manufactures reached the indicated level."

The great contemporary value of the report was not so much its prediction as its source. This was, indeed, the voice of business speaking. It was an optimistic voice, but it was based on research and it obviously was not propaganda. No other business organization had yet spoken in these terms. And because in the less than three years of its existence CED had indeed become, in the words of *Time* magazine, "a voice of authority," and because it was known intimately in small and large centers through the grass-roots work of its Field Division, the report struck home. Only a few questioned its accuracy or validity.

Business Week was quick to point out, in a friendly editorial, that, in using its mathematical procedure, a difference of one hour in the factory work week assumed (CED assumed that the 1939 work week of 37.7 hours would prevail rather than the 1941 work week of 40.6 hours) would affect the total employment figure by more than 1,000,000. It also pointed out that a difference of only .005 per cent in the estimated ratio between factory and total employment would affect the total by more than 1,000,000. "Thus," it concluded, "building a total employment figure from the forecast of manufacturing output by using actual 1941 conditions [1941, the magazine recalled, was a "rather special, arms-boom year"] instead of those which CED assumes, gives a total of about 46,500,000 jobs, instead of 53,500,-000—or an unemployment figure of ten million instead of one or three million."

Toward the end of the year, when it began to appear that the specter of unemployment was not stalking the land, the *New York Times* said in an editorial: "Government experts are reported to have admitted that they overestimated the number of unemployed which would develop because of reconversion. Now they estimate that not more than 5 million rather than 8 million will be seeking employment in the spring of 1946." After reviewing the bad guessing of some officials, the newspaper said that their estimates "were more than 3 times as large as actually turned out to be the case." And President Truman (who incidentally never included CED in his vigorous attacks on Big Business) admitted to the Conference of Mayors that "so far the unemployment situation has not been so serious or drastic as was originally anticipated" by his own advisors—or by Walter Reuther who, two months after the publication of the Marketing Committee's report, had declared that the prosperity predicted for the United States would be "a prosperity for everybody but the people" and had warned that unless a 30 per cent wage boost were granted "this brief boom will collapse" and "carry the nation back to a depression with 19,000,000 unemployed."

Commenting three years afterward upon the various postwar plans of business, one economist, Leo Barnes, who found the CED forecast to be among the best, remarked: "Unfortunately, not a single link in this chain of reasoning is sound. If the correct assumptions as revealed by actual developments are substituted for the incorrect ones employed by CED, it turns out that the manufacturing output forecast by American business for the year beginning September 1946 would actually have provided jobs for forty-six million persons and joblessness for thirteen million."

Twelve months after V-J Day the actual employment figure was 57,050,000. From this grew the myth that the Committee for Economic Development missed hitting it on the nose by 50,000! Of course, this was not so. It had suggested 57 million as a possible upper limit; but it had also *suggested* 51 million as a lower limit. Its actual prediction was 53,448,000. Thus, at its best guess, it was 3,602,000 out of the way.

With the publication of this pamphlet, there were many who felt that CED's work was done. The war was ended. Business was once again on its own, as war order after war order was suddenly canceled. The postwar years were now the present, and large-scale unemployment was not stalking the land. Thousands of individual businessmen, executives of large and small enterprises, among them some of CED's trustees, now felt able to face the problems of the new peacetime. But those who would return to the prewar patterns failed to reckon with the determination of those few businessmen who had discovered the value of research, who saw in the partnership between businessmen and scholars a means to keep the economy growing.

FIVE

Business Gropes for Goals

WHILE MOST businessmen looked upon the Committee for Economic Development only as an emergency war measure designed to stir the business community to action, there were two, at least, who had a larger vision from the very outset. Paul Hoffman and William Benton saw it as a permanent and valuable projection of that marshaling of businessmen and theoretical economists which had never been far from their thinking since 1939.

Benton had undertaken the task of building up the original Research Committee of businessmen and the equally important group of scholars known as the Research Advisory Board. To find the right men he traveled thousands of miles, visited no less than forty colleges and universities, consulted with scores of leading businessmen, government officials, and professional economists in and out of the government. His aim was to have as "liberal" a group as possible, with one or two who did not fit exactly into this category in order to give it that balance necessary to make it acceptable to the business community.

At the very beginning Ralph Flanders had been his choice as chairman and he sought to find businessmen and social scientists who would work with this dynamic Yankee. Flanders' own

knowledge of the economic world and its personalities was wide
and he was in constant communication with Benton during the
latter's long and arduous search for talent.

When Benton approached Thurman Arnold for advice the
New Deal trust buster gave him two criteria to work on: "Don't
touch the orthodox type of scholar. They wrecked the Temporary National Economic Commission (TNEC) by disagreement"; and, "Don't sell yourself down the river with fellows
who don't know how the economy works." Following this
advice Benton finally assembled a Research Advisory Board
whose strength and diversity were to contribute materially to
CED's early won reputation for objectivity and integrity. The
minutes of CED trustee meetings are replete with statements by
businessmen-trustees who found association with the advisors a
stimulating adventure. For many of them it was their first contact with academicians and they discovered that they were not
the "long-haired professors who had never had to meet a pay-
roll," as cartoons often made them appear.

Of the scholars on the advisory panel, Hoffman was later to
say, "I don't think there has ever been a group so carefully
checked and double-checked. Of course, we were not just seeking scientists who would agree with businessmen. Our objective
was to find men who had the highest standing for professional
competence and intellectual integrity."

Heading the Research Advisory Board was Sumner Slichter.
If *Times*'s description of him as a "Wisconsin liberal—a conservative liberal that does not go off half-cocked"—was correct,
Slichter was just the sort of economist that the new committee
needed. The brown-eyed, white-haired professor, already a
prolific writer on economics, was less known at that time as an
economic prognosticator than as an expert in labor-management
problems. He had a reputation for objectivity; his writings were
as welcome in the columns of the *Atlantic Monthly* as in the
New Republic. Since CED was dedicated to the objective of full
employment his presence was understandable. Perhaps his most

forceful stand was his opinion, expressed several years earlier, that a strong labor movement was necessary, among other reasons, if only to compel business to raise its own standards of efficiency. Although CED itself was quietly to accept much Keynesian philosophy, Slichter, strangely enough, was not professedly of the Keynes school, especially that part which expressed too great a reliance on governmental "interference" in the conduct of private enterprise. He was a low tariff advocate.

As far as possible Benton acted upon the advice of Chancellor Day of Cornell, one of his close advisors, and sought young men for the board. Robert de B. Calkins, newly come to Columbia from the West Coast, was thirty-nine; Neil Jacoby, of the University of Chicago and fresh from a year on a special assignment for the National Bureau of Economic Research, was thirty-three; Ralph Young, William I. Myers of Cornell, Theodore Schultz, and Harold D. Lasswell were all young men.

Working with these academic experts were eleven businessmen, all carefully screened for their interest in research and their willingness to devote time and effort to committee work. Besides Flanders, there were William L. Batt, president of SKF Industries, Philadelphia; Donald David, dean of the Harvard Graduate School of Business and director of several corporations; Max Epstein, chairman of the board of the General American Transportation Company of Chicago; Beardsley Ruml, treasurer of R. H. Macy Company; William Benton; Chester C. Davis, president of the Federal Reserve Bank of St. Louis; Paul Hoffman; Eric Johnston, president of Brown-Johnston Company, Spokane, and newly elected head of the United States Chamber of Commerce; Charles E. Wilson, president of General Electric Company; and S. Bayard Colgate, chairman of the board of Colgate-Palmolive-Peet corporation.

A description of these men at work survives in a short speech which Neil H. Jacoby gave to the Citizens' Board of the University of Chicago toward the end of the first year: an "eyewitness account of a battle of words and ideas" during a three-day meeting of research committeemen, staff, and Research Advisory Board.

"This verbal engagement," Dr. Jacoby recounted, "was fought in the University Club of New York. At the moment the territory in dispute is postwar Federal taxation policy. Leading the assault is Professor Harold Groves of Wisconsin, one of Professor Yntema's research staff, armed with a powerful report on tax reform.* Professor Groves has just won a strategic position.

"Momentarily the front is quiet. Then Professor Groves lays down another barrage. He proposes that net capital gains should be included in the taxable income of persons and treated exactly like other income, because a personal income tax should reach the *total* annual increase in each person's economic power, and this includes net capital gains. Instantly the battle of ideas flares anew. For an hour the crossfire of criticism is heavy. The opposition argues that capital gains are different from salaries, interest, or dividends; that the Groves proposal will reduce job-giving and investment; that the British policy of ignoring capital gains and losses and taxing only income of a recurring nature is the correct one. But Professor Groves and his cohorts steadily hold to their principles. They point to grave practical difficulties in administering the British law. Finally, Professor Groves wins his position, though not without taking heavy blows. The battle of ideas moves on to new lines—other tax policies, government fiscal policies, wage and labor policy, international economic policy, policies to encourage new and small business, policies to maintain competition in all markets."

Meetings such as this one were held at two-month intervals in New York and Chicago, where Dr. Yntema maintained his headquarters. "Because every man has heavy wartime responsibilities that fill his business hours," Neil Jacoby recited, "the meetings

---

* Published (June, 1944) by CED as a research study, *Production, Jobs and Taxes: Postwar Revision of the Federal Tax System to Help Achieve Higher Production and More Jobs.* This was the first research study of ten published in the first three years of CED.

are held on week-ends. From Saturday morning to the following Sunday afternoon—with no Saturday evening off—the sessions continue. These are not conventions, complete with pep-talks, floor shows, and hangovers. They are intensely hard-working meetings, in which every man deeply feels the difficulty and importance of his task. I have never attended round table conferences where the level of discussion is consistently as high. The talk is utterly frank and pointed, with no quarter given or asked. Each participant finds that his views are exposed to sharp analysis. Those ideas that survive are noted by the research staff. In this way complex approaches to specific questions are devised."

This close relationship of give and take between the businessmen and the professors proved that the two old antagonists could get together for their mutual benefit. What Jacoby fancifully called the "bridging of the moat between the ivory tower and the market place," perhaps even more than the resulting policies or learned studies, was the great accomplishment of CED in its first year of existence.

Early in 1944 Carle Conway, head of Continental Can Company, had reported to the trustees that some of the more conservative businessmen whom he approached in his drive to raise funds for CED were "afraid of the possible political implications they think might develop in our program." He gave as an example one of the nation's largest publicly owned utilities which would not contribute for this reason, although its management was in sympathy with CED's aims. Although only one policy statement had been issued at this time, "Some people," Conway said, "think we scatter our shots too much. Others are afraid of our getting into the field of tax policy."

Another trustee spoke then of the "violent emotions that revolve around free trade and protective tariff question" and wondered if, in these fields, CED could maintain that objectivity of which it was so proud. To this another replied, "If you could have heard Calvin Hoover's initial presentation of his international report you would certainly realize what an objective approach we are following in this field."

Years later in recalling this period Dr. Calvin Hoover, the noted economist of Duke University, said, "The series of conferences as the study took shape were of the greatest use in enabling me to understand the changed attitudes of industrialists about international trade and the tariff. I believe, too, that the industrial executives who participated in those long discussions got a widened and deepened understanding of the role played in international trade by institutions such as the International Bank and Fund and some understanding of the assumptions upon which the doctrine of free trade rests, together with a realization of the extent to which these assumptions were no longer entirely valid. They came to recognize, instead, that we have a series of national economies which are not fully competitive in the old sense with relatively inflexible national price levels and in some cases with economies partially and even wholly state-controlled.

"I think that the mutual acquaintanceship of academic economists and of industrial executives which developed as the industrialists learned, for example, that deficit financing was not always sinful, while the academicians got renewed evidence that industrialists were neither by instinct nor by inheritance invariably oligopolists with respect to prices nor monopsonists with regard to wages, was of great value."

The reaction of the industrialist to the CED process is to be found in this remark by Ralph Flanders in 1944:

"You can take it for granted that I would not be neglecting my own business, as I am, for this research work, if I did not feel deeply that without the types of policies this program is working towards, everything else that business may try to do will fail. You ought to realize that this research program is an exceedingly delicate operation. We were faced at the start with distrust from the academicians, from labor, and from small business, from big business and banking. I think we have pretty well dispelled the distrust among the professional economists. We can meet the hurdles of these other forms of distrust. . . ."

The process of mutual education by the businessman and the scholar headed quickly into its most critical test. When the trustees gathered at Hot Springs, Virginia, in mid-September, 1944, those who believed in long-range research were confronted directly by those who regarded CED as a wartime emergency agency, created for a specific purpose, and to be dissolved when the postwar employment problem disappeared. Perhaps Sidney Weinberg, a partner in Goldman, Sachs, and one of CED's most influential trustees and effective fund-raisers, best posed the issue when he told the gathering at the Homestead that he had come there to "set a definite maturity date on the existence of CED."

When Weinberg raised this question he was surrounded not only by other budget-minded businessmen like himself but also by members of the Research Committee and the Research Advisory Board and the advocates of mutual education. They went to work now on Sidney Weinberg.

With Ralph Flanders, intense, serious, and persuasive as ever, leading the way, aided and abetted by Theodore Yntema, head of the research staff, and such businessmen-scholars as Beardsley Ruml, Donald David, and Raymond Rubicam, he began to change his mind. Between them they told him of the astonishingly small amount of money that American business was actually spending for research in the United States at that time; how the research process, if it were to serve a useful purpose, was time-consuming and exacting; and what the research then under way was trying to do.

Donald David pleaded for the continuance of a long-range research program. Paul Hoffman pointed out that if American business had spent perhaps 5 million dollars on "policy research" in the 1920's "we might have saved at least $50 billion of the $200 billion of national production lost during the depression." And William Benton argued that the committee should start raising more money, especially for long-range research. In the face of these arguments Weinberg and others were convinced that research was the solid core of CED and should be continued after the war.

At this meeting there was also much soul searching over what the group actually was trying to accomplish. Early in 1943, Paul Hoffman had said that the committee was dedicated to the belief that "all measures of government, of business, and of labor that interfere with expanding employment should be challenged." But, in a preface to the first "statement on national policy," Ralph Flanders had been more cautious. CED's purpose, he wrote, was "to stimulate and assist American business to make the maximum contribution that is possible *on a sound business basis* to high employment and production after the war."

As might be expected, Beardsley Ruml had another, and perhaps loftier definition of its aims, even when limited to the field of high productive employment in a free society: "The increase of human understanding and . . . the application of economic wisdom for human welfare." Ruml agreed with Hoffman's and Benton's original conception of a joint venture of the business and academic mind when he said that CED would draw its success in "combining fruitfully *experience, thought,* and *action,* a process that must precede the increase of knowledge in any field."

Whatever the purpose, the group was told by its by-laws that: "All research is to be thoroughly objective in character, and the approach in each instance is to be from the standpoint of the general welfare and not from that of any special political or economic group."

William Benton volunteered to try to set down on paper an exposition of the basic economic philosophy of those tenets on which the committee functioned. He went at the task of setting down the assumptions and convictions of CED "with such energy and enthusiasm as I have seldom seen devoted to such a thankless job," according to Professor Yntema. At least forty drafts were written by Benton and torn to shreds by staff, economic advisors, and fellow trustees before *The Economics of a Free Society: A Declaration of American Business Policy*, with its twelve articles of faith, was completed.*

In order to understand why *The Economics of a Free Society* caused at least a ripple of excitement and much raising of eyebrows on the business right, we must go back to January, 1944. In his annual message to Congress, at the beginning of another election year, President Roosevelt, pausing momentarily in the prosecution of the war, had eloquently restated his belief that "true individual freedom cannot exist without economic security and independence," and had then gone on to present what he called an Economic Bill of Rights, designed to implement this truism. Essentially this was a summing up of the domestic social and economic achievements of the New Deal and a promise of their continuance. It was a calm and far from radical defense and so rational that Governor Dewey, the Republican candidate, kept finding himself in agreement with it during the campaign.

As a matter of fact, Governor Dewey forced the economic issue of postwar employment into the campaign. "We must have full employment," he said at Seattle in September, reiterating his June acceptance speech in which he had said, "We Republicans are agreed that full employment shall be a first objective of national policy. . . . Government's first job in the peacetime years ahead will be to see that conditions exist which promote widespread job opportunities in private enterprise."

Vice President Wallace, whose *Sixty Million Jobs* was not to be published until the following year, was alone among Democrats to stress full employment. President Roosevelt directed his campaign oratory to the lofty plane of the war effort until Dewey's stressing of the job theme prompted Democratic strategists to urge him to deliver at least one important speech on

---

* It was published as a supplementary paper, rather than as a policy statement, in December, 1944, following its appearance in full in the October, 1944, issue of *Fortune*. As a supplementary paper, of course, it did not have the endorsement of CED or of its research committee; but it was generally accepted as having been approved in principle by the top leaders of CED.

domestic issues. Dewey's taking up of this subject was good politics, if nothing more. Everyone of course was "for" full employment: at least nobody could be expected to endorse a program of postwar depression!

Economics of a Free Society began with the declaration that the good of all is superior to the economic interest of any group, a declaration thoroughly consistent with the Constitution, common sense, and the by-laws of CED. The economic system, it went on, is but a tool for achieving the common good. The economic system which was chosen by the American people is the free enterprise system which, when it functions properly, permits the maximum freedom to the individual consistent with the common good.

In a democracy there is room for both private enterprise and public enterprise. Beyond the limit "of private enterprise . . . to serve the common good," government enterprise is necessary. Government must devise and enforce "reasonably stable rules that will encourage private, voluntary enterprise." A climate in which "new, small and independent business can be conceived and born, can grow and prosper" is essential to free enterprise.

Business must be allowed to grow and become great, provided that "the power that comes with size is not allowed to stifle competition."

Wage earners need the right to bargain collectively. Special-interest groups arise from the "natural tendency of man to organize," but none should be allowed to "use their power to further monopolistic practices, cartels or other special interests that check the rise of the country's standard of living."

Prolonged and serious depressions cannot be accepted as "natural and irremediable phenomena." Government must establish fiscal, monetary, and other policies that will help prevent "the fever of inflation and the paralysis of deflation and depression." When "free enterprise . . . fails to meet the imperative need for high employment and productivity," government must take steps to expand "private employment and needed public employment."

In order to protect the individual against "the adjustments inevitable in a changing and developing economy," government should widen the coverage of social security, unemployment insurance, and old-age pensions.

Private enterprise is the best system because it can and does develop a high and rapidly rising level of living; because it assures an American prosperity so vital to world prosperity and world peace; because it fosters "native capacity, ambition and resourcefulness of individuals"; and because it protects personal freedom and well-being from "the dangers inherent in too great a concentration of either private or public power."

This was, in 1944, the true voice of liberal conservatism—using both words in their proper sense.* The flexibility, thoughtfulness, and the clarity of the document set its author and those who subscribed to it off from the fundamentalist right, while it did not swing them very far to the left.

William Benton, in an address made a decade later, recalled that his statement went through forty-four drafts and much debate, resulting in "a few . . . ideas (that) seemed shocking at the time to many businessmen." He cited as most distasteful the "place for public enterprise" in the economy, collective bargaining, and that clause espousing legislative responsibility for fiscal and monetary policies to combat inflation, deflation and depression. "In retrospect," he told the Young Presidents' National Convention, "it seems clear to me that the greatest single service rendered by the CED has been the education of its members from the business community in politics and economics. Most of them however, . . . have remained loyal to the Republican

---

* "Liberal conservatives make counterproposals to the promises of the Left and accept the new dimensions in government with little rancor or regret. Some of them have been known to say a kind word for the 'purposes' if not the 'methods' of Mr. Roosevelt."—Clinton Rossiter, *Conservatism in America*, New York, 1955, p. 184.

Party—although many of these . . . are somewhat suspect within it."

Despite the success in stimulating job opportunities, producing respected research and policy recommendations, and articulating goals, the fate of the Committee for Economic Development became an acute problem for its trustees after the surrender of Japan. Under the terms of their gentlemen's agreement with the National Association of Manufacturers and the United States Chamber of Commerce, both of whom wanted no rival business organization cluttering up the scene which they had so long dominated, the time had come for the wartime emergency organization to close up shop.

Heartrending though it might be to the hard core of CED trustees who had devoted so much of their time, money, and labor to the organization, there seemed no alternative. As far as the Field Development Division was concerned, with its far-flung setup from coast to coast, there appeared to be no reason for, or possibility of, keeping CED going any longer.

But was this also true of the Research Division? This was a question not readily resolved. To William Benton the closing down of the research end of CED was unthinkable, for it would mean the end of his dream before it had wholly proved its worth. To Paul Hoffman it posed a dilemma. He wavered between the arguments for and against the complete dissolution of the committee which he not only headed but of which, in the public eye at least, he was the founder. Both they and the men who had made up that hard-working and stubborn crowd, whose efforts had produced three outstanding and widely approved statements on national policy affecting the future of the economic world, were distressed.

To dissolve CED would probably mean there would be no more of those famous meetings in which professional economists sat down to deal with reality across the table from businessmen who, to use Walter Bagehot's well-known phrase, had "lived all their lives in an atmosphere of uncertainties and doubt, where nothing is very clear." In the three years in which the CED process had worked, many doubts and uncertainties had been cleared up, both for the academicians and for the businessmen who had jointly subjected themselves to this process of immolation of preconceived ideas and fixed predilections at the altar of approachable truth.

But a businessman's word must be kept and so, although painfully, it was decided to end the great experiment. First the Field Division must go, and then the Research Division, still deep in work-in-progress, must clear its desks and utter its last statement on national policy. But ending CED did not turn out to be as easy as it seemed. There was reluctance on the part of several trustees to close down a going concern.

Acting on the theory that it would be economically wasteful completely to disband the active organization of community, county, and state CED's, so painfully established in 2,947 places from Maine to California, and which might well be counted upon to carry on their work of stimulating the economic growth of the country, C. Scott Fletcher set himself to the task of finding a place in which they might fit.

Fletcher, with his proved genius for organization, worked out an intricate plan whereby the nucleus of CED's Field Development Division would be absorbed by the United States Chamber of Commerce. The Chamber would also assume the responsibility for distributing the products of the Research Division, which would then be maintained as a separate entity. This plan called for the merging of Field Development with a new committee to be known as the National Community Development Committee (CDC) of the United States Chamber of Commerce. Its purpose would be to stimulate and assist local chambers of commerce to organize over-all community development committees which would "bring together under business leadership all segments of the economy for the purpose of building a better community and a higher standard of living for all."

Fletcher felt that "if we want to avoid industrial strife on the home front, we must encourage a cooperative attitude on the part of business rather than one of isolationism." His proposed CDC would instill in the minds of all citizens that its objective was "not to chase the will-o-the-wisp of a perfect social order, national or international, which is imposed from the top down," but to attempt to bring "our problems down to the size which our minds can encompass and begin to build solidly from the ground up."

"If we, as a nation," he wrote, expressing an unproved theory dear to the business community, "can solve our smaller local problems properly, there is every reason to believe that many of our larger national and international problems will take care of themselves. If, on the other hand, our business leaders attempt to take advantage of the opportunities of the future by advocating short-sighted and narrowly selfish policies, there is no doubt that we shall witness a brief and violent reaction which will be succeeded by an even more violent swing in the opposite direction. In other words, if business through its leadership community by community and by cooperation with all segments in the community shows that it is moderate and far-sighted in its demands, then there is every reason to believe we will be in for a long era of stability, good feeling, and prosperity."

Paul Hoffman entertained honest doubts about the propriety of continuing CED, but he was impressed with the possibilities inherent in Fletcher's plan. The working out of means of assimilation with the USCC (of which Eric Johnston, an original and active trustee of CED, was still president) which Fletcher enclosed with his fervent plea, seemed feasible and easy to accomplish at that time. In September, Fletcher presented it to a meeting of the Business Advisory Council—the same group which in the winter of 1942 had listened to the Upgren-Department of Commerce report that set in motion the founding of CED.

Eric Johnston was so impressed that he invited him to repeat it to the Staff of the United States Chamber of Commerce the

following week. In the meantime he approached Paul Hoffman to explore the possibility of putting this or a similar plan into
effect. Hoffman properly backed away, saying it was entirely up
to the CED board of trustees but that he would suggest to
them the possibility of such an arrangement if the Chamber was
"really interested." President Johnston, who was soon to leave
the Chamber to head the Motion Picture Association, arranged
for Fletcher to tell the board of directors of the Chamber about
his plan.

As a result, the executive committee of the USCC was authorized to suggest to the CED trustees "the taking over by the
Chamber of the Field Division." At an all-day meeting the CED
trustees appointed a twelve-man committee which had full
power to act on the future of CED. This followed a vigorous
discussion in which Paul Hoffman pointed out the accomplish-
ments of the Field Division and the need to maintain the "tremendous potentiality of the leadership on Main Street." He
approved the plan, declaring that if CED attempted to keep the
Field Division in operation it would be "a withering process,"
whereas it could flourish as a function of the Chamber of Commerce. Hoffman saw, however, that while the Chamber was the
logical organization to take over the field program, it needed, as
he said, to "broaden its vision." Not only would the community
CEDs necessitate this but would assist in bringing it about. The
plan, he showed, could not be "carried on by the Chamber acting
as a Chamber" but only as an over-all community council, as
CED had operated in communities during the war.

The special committee later met with the Chamber's executive
committee and proposed that the Chamber abolish its own Community Economic Councils, substitute the CED plan, "borrow"
Fletcher for a year to get it going, and accept, if necessary, a
financial grant from CED to help launch the project. After two
meetings the Executive Committee of the Chamber rejected the
CED proposal. This negative action was approved by the board
of directors, but at the earnest persuasion of Clarence Francis and

the late Gibson Carey, both of whom were CED trustees as well as members of the USCC, they agreed to postpone action and explore the proposal further. Clarence Francis then arranged a meeting between Eric Johnston and Otto Seyforth, as Chamber representatives, and Paul Hoffman, who worked out an agreement after amending the original plan to meet certain Chamber objections. It then appeared as if an agreement had been reached. But staff members of the Chamber of Commerce, undoubtedly fearful that they would be subordinated or removed as a result of the "merger," raised objections which were supported by the executive committee. On January 31, the board of directors politely but firmly turned down the plan. There was nothing to do but dissolve the Field Division. When the CED trustees met on February 12 they ordered this done within thirty days.

At this meeting the trustees heard Paul Hoffman say:

"Although the Field Division has met the assignment which it took on, the Research Division has as yet met its task only in a partial manner. . . . The work of the Research Division has to date largely been devoted to problems of the transition period. There are still a number of important studies under way dealing with long-range problems—*maintaining* high employment. We cannot solve our problems by ignorant change or ignorant opposition to change. The further studies of the Research Division will take possibly two or three years to complete. It may be wise to expand and take up other questions, such as labor policies and monopolies. This has become a pressure group economy and we must learn how to make a pressure group economy function in the general public interest. . . ."

Just before the trustees voted unanimously to continue the work of the Research Division "for another 18 months, perhaps as long as three years," Paul Hoffman read parts of a letter from Harrison Jones, chairman of the board of the Coca Cola Corporation:

"The penalty of great vision and unusual and unique accomplishment is the inability to find successors with the dream and the energy to perpetuate it. I am for calling it a day. I am for not attempting to get any other organization to handle it. I think the Field Development end should not be perpetuated by us. As to the other thing—research: it should not die—must not die—that must go on!"

SIX

A Postwar Tax Policy

IN RECENT years Beardsley Ruml has often been called the "national idea man," but back in 1944 he had only just come into public prominence as the father of the pay-as-you-go income tax plan. His pioneering, however, had begun long before and his little-known achievements already had led to his being called by Robert Hutchins the "founder of social sciences in America."

Ruml has always blamed his hatred of physical labor for his intellectual achievements. Even in high school in Cedar Rapids, Iowa, he got into the habit of attacking his school work with wild energy in the hope of getting so far ahead that he could relax for a year. This was one of his few erroneous theories. The more successfully he avoided physical activity the more he uncovered intellectual curiosities that he felt must be pursued. This led him to the writing of poetry and plays at Dartmouth and into a Ph.D. degree in intelligence measuring at the University of Chicago.

At the age of twenty-seven, Ruml was given the job of thinking up ways to spend the 74 million dollars John D. Rockefeller, Jr. had placed in the Laura Spelman Rockefeller Memorial Fund. There he argued for and won authorization for spending the first large funds to be devoted in this country to social science research. In 1930 he was named dean of social sciences at the University of Chicago and four years later moved into business to become the treasurer of Macy's. Meanwhile, he had originated the farmers' protective tariff, otherwise known as the domestic allotment plan, which President Roosevelt later picked up as the basis for the Agricultural Adjustment Act.

His instinct for challenging established ideas and cross-examining everything led him into evolving a completely new accounting system for Macy's, even though he had never studied accounting. His business success, which he dismissed as the mere result of "creative ignorance," attracted attention and he was soon a director and then chairman of the Federal Reserve Bank of New York.

He conceived the withholding method for income tax collection in 1942 and presented it to the United States Treasury Department. Told that its adoption was a "political impossibility," he applied his conviction that the average impossibility is a pushover, waged a public battle for his idea, and succeeded in selling it.

Dr. James Rowland Angell, former president of Yale, once said that Ruml had the remarkable faculty of taking nothing for granted and of approaching every problem as if it were something entirely new. This was the faculty he put to work on the postwar tax problem.

Early in 1943 he and his colleagues, working under Ralph Flanders' direction on the Research Committee of CED, had commissioned Dean C. E. Griffin, head of the School of Business Administration at the University of Michigan, to set up a series of research studies under the general heading of "Taxation and Business: Studies of Incentives for Business Enterprise and the Impact of Taxation on these Incentives." For the study on postwar tax revision, Dean Griffin chose Harold M. Groves, Professor of Economics at the University of Wisconsin, with the added help of Henry C. Simons from the University of Chicago and William A. Paton from the University of Michigan.

This and other projects directed toward the same issue all began producing results in the summer of 1944. At Harvard, Alvin Hansen and Harvey Perloff completed work on their study on *State and Local Finance in the National Economy*, which included a plan for postwar tax reform. A group of businessmen in Minneapolis and St. Paul published the "Twin Cities Plan" for tax reform. And Beardsley Ruml, working in the National Planning Association as well as with the Research Committee of CED, produced with Christian Sonne the Ruml-Sonne plan. And in June, 1944, Senator Walter George's Postwar Planning Committee issued its report in which a prominent place was given to the need for tax revision.

This same week, Professor Groves's short, 168-page study, written in clear, understandable language and entitled *Production, Jobs and Taxes* was published. Although the help of the businessmen members of the CED Research Committee was acknowledged, the book's foreword made clear that academic freedom had been jealously guarded and that the conclusions were the scholar's own. Ralph Flanders added that the businessmen had drawn heavily upon the research conducted under Professor Groves's direction but would publish their own conclusions in a separate statement of policy recommendations.

The hardy, self-made and largely self-taught Vermonter knew whereof he spoke because he ran CED's Research Committee with an iron and relentless hand.

"Ralph Flanders is from Vermont," a magazine writer explained, "and natives of that state, as everyone knows, do not speak until they have thought long and carefully. As with Vermonters so with CED. Before it whispers an opinion it commissions a full-dress and professionally competent study of the whole subject, usually getting an outside authority to write a book. Its own conclusions are issued later in the form of a pamphlet, or 'policy' statement.

"In framing this statement it assembles the dozen-odd businessmen of its research committee (who by then have done their homework on the over-all study) along with a dozen advisors from the universities, guests from the C.I.O. and A.F. of L., etc. Few groups of such size and diverse opinions have learned so well how to thread their way through complex issues. Chairman Flanders explains and persuades while Beardsley Ruml acts as a kind of intellectual traffic cop. Anyone who tries to detour into double talk or feeble compromise incurs the considerable wrath of the considerable Ruml. If there are any cliché experts in regular attendance, they have been thoroughly intimidated."

While Flanders was explaining and Ruml was guiding the intellectual traffic, the writing was being done mainly by Harry Scherman who, like Ruml, had acquired a fortune and a national reputation by successfully challenging an established notion. The notion in this case was that the American public was allergic to books. He was convinced that it was not the books that were at fault but the scarcity and inconvenience of bookstores. By the time he established the Book-of-the-Month Club in 1926 to sell books by direct mail, he had already made his point by selling 40,000 copies of the classics in "The Little Leather Library" through chain variety stores, drugstores, and direct mail. His genius for selling books through the mail was not allowed to overcome his love for writing about economics. In 1942 he had written an article on money and credit for the *Saturday Evening Post* called "Invisible Greenbacks" that remains to this day one of the most widely reprinted magazine articles. He expanded it into a book, *The Promises Men Live By*, which is still "must" reading in many college economics courses.

Even with this talent at work, the businessmen of CED must have been a little astonished at the reception given their first major policy statement, *A Postwar Federal Tax Plan for High Employment*, when it appeared in August, 1944. The *Nation* declared that of all the plans by businessmen or business groups the CED recommendations "are most deserving of close study." Even the *New Republic* greeted it with respect. *Fortune*, in a lengthy analysis of all the tax programs then in the public eye, singled out the CED plan as the most progressive and impressive one.

Beardsley Ruml, who has sat through most of the fiscal policy statements hammered out by CED, has recalled that this was "by all odds the most difficult to produce." Its recommendations may have been no more controversial than those of later statements, but the committee was new, the technical staff untested by CED standards, which were in their very first stages of development. In a way, everyone was groping in the dark; nevertheless, after eighteen months of groping ("no one knows how many meetings, formal or informal, were held," Ruml has said) the eleven businessmen, each with a right to state a wholly differing point of view on any detail or even on the statement as a whole, reached substantially unanimous agreement on the controversial subject. What is more, they laid down certain lines which were to be followed in future years, and provided a foundation for later statements of policy to meet realities that would have appeared fantastic in the fiscal year of 1944.

The statement opened with an expression of grave concern over the probable size of the federal budget in the first postwar years. Although it realized that any estimate would be an uncertain one, the statement was positive in its assertion that, after the war, the total federal expenditures could not be less than between 16 and 18 billion dollars annually (not including social security and retirement of the debt).* In that war year (which had yet to see the launching of the Battle of the Bulge or the beginnings of victory in the Pacific) there was no way of predicting the dawn of the atomic age, the uneasiness of the peace, the rift with our wartime ally, Russia, the cold war, Korea, or the extent of national defense.

Having warned of this huge, inevitable jump in the cost of national government, the CED statement presented three major objectives. The first, which was basic to its entire argument, was that any realistic postwar tax system must impose the least possi-

* The Ruml-Sonne and Twin Cities plans reached the same figures.

ble restriction upon an expansion of production and employment. Second, the federal tax must be fair among persons. And third, it must be adequate to instill justifiable confidence in the integrity of the federal government, the soundness of the dollar, and the safety of the federal debt as an investment.

In order to meet these objectives it divided its program into five parts: (1) one-half the needed revenue should come from a graduated personal income tax; (2) the excise taxes then in force should be lightened; (3) business taxes should be lightened; (4) inequities should be removed from the tax structure; (5) when a satisfactory level of employment and production was reached, federal taxation should be heavy enough to make possible substantial reduction in the national debt.

CED's businessman's committee in 1944 was convinced that the income tax was the most equitable tax, far less repressive than a sales tax or a profits tax. It was fairest because it was best adjusted according to the ability to pay, because it was clearly evident where the burden fell, and because, by causing widespread personal concern, it would tend toward bringing about more governmental economy and efficiency.

Excise taxes, perhaps necessary in war time, were wrong primarily because they imposed an unfair burden on persons of low income. Furthermore they raised prices and adversely affected the volume of employment, particularly in mass-production industries. However, the historic excise taxes on liquor and tobacco, and perhaps on gasoline, should be retained, for they provided a heavy and stable source of revenue easy and cheap to administer.

It was in the field of the corporation tax that the CED statement trod most controversially on treacherous territory. It was CED's opinion that all taxes were paid by individuals; therefore, the corporation merely conceals the division of the burden as between stockholders, workers, and consumers. Taxes on profits, it argued, were damaging to employment because they weaken the "profit incentive" and take earnings that might be reinvested

(CED did not guarantee that they *would* be) in production, and because they limit the capacity of management to increase wages and lower prices. The inequity of "taxing the same income at two points" disturbed CED then, as it does today.

The statement spelled out some of the other inequities which it was convinced should be removed. These were: the exemption from taxation of state and local securities; the failure of family exemptions then in force to apply to the normal income tax of 3 per cent; the failure to provide for the carrying forward of business losses; the failure to allow the averaging of individual incomes for tax purposes when the income varied in significant amounts from year to year; and the use of "incentive taxation," or the attempt to stimulate enterprise by special tax differentials.

Whether or not this actually was, as *Life* exultantly exclaimed, "something wholly new in United States tax policy," it was a fresh and invigorating statement to emanate from a business-man's group. Some of its faults were quickly pointed out by CED's friends and enemies. Even then it was obvious to critics that CED had grossly underestimated postwar military expenditures. Some right-wing critics felt that its forthright rejection of a sales tax was wrong. But there was, in well-informed publications, unusual agreement that this very stand lent strength to CED's statement, for its proposals would not only remove the chief aggressive aspects of the then current tax system but would provide a cushion against a postwar depression by assuring a higher level of buying power for that part of the population where buying habits are most sensitive to unemployment and cyclic changes.

It was when CED proposed the elimination of all corporate taxes—except a single flat tax corresponding to the basic normal tax on individual incomes—and urged that the money received by individuals in dividends be exempt from normal taxes that (in the words of the *Nation*) it trod "on more questionable grounds." But in this respect the CED statement was milder than the Twin-Cities suggestion of a two-thirds reduction on the corporate load and the Ruml-Sonne proposal, which urged the complete abolition of income taxes on corporations.

And so the argument raged, with some critics reaching for Lord Keynes to slay the CED argument with his theory that it was the "oversaving" by American business corporations which was one of the major causes of the world depression in 1929. America, it must be remembered, was quite widely depression-minded in 1944 (in spite of CED's widespread propaganda that prosperity should and could be the postwar promise!) and Keynes, rightly or wrongly interpreted, was the most influential source of much economic thinking at that time.

Many now felt that the CED plan would accentuate the pressure to withhold dividends, because earnings would be larger, thus threatening to force the individual stockholder's tax into even higher brackets. A high corporation tax, these critics felt, would force a large part of the national earnings back into circulation, and this would have a greater effect in directly supporting employment and business activity than the elimination of the corporation tax.

There was one other valid criticism of the CED statement, which found its best expression in *Time*. Despite its "resolute insistence upon a balanced budget annually CED would accept an increase in the Federal debt 'under clear conditions of slump in industry and trade,' " the news magazine said. The statement maintained that its tax schedules would make a sizable debt retirement possible at a 140-billion-dollar national income, and a balanced budget at a lower level. But, inasmuch as the revenue yield of the CED tax plan was calculated to average only about 18 billion dollars at a 140-billion-dollar national income, "it looks as if CED were prepared to accept deficit financing when national income falls below $140 billion." Or, as *Time*'s sister *Life* put it: "They aim to balance the budget only when the economy is balanced first."

But, in the final analysis, the sins of omission or commission in the CED statement did not really matter. What did matter was the fact that an important group of businessmen, whose words were already being carefully listened to in high places of government, had issued a clear, informed, and intelligent plea for tax revision and tax reform as necessary prerequisites to successful attainment of full and productive employment. It was a plan in many respects "far more satisfactory than our present (1944) system of taxation, which rests so heavily on the low-income group." In its minor way it was a historic document. For with its publication CED took its place as an organization that was determined to find, through research, practical ways and means of attaining its high aims of high employment and high production in a free society.

SEVEN

Full Employment

As 1945 dawned the economic fate of the United States and its people in the postwar era was becoming a dominant theme. In his Economic Bill of Rights, President Roosevelt had sounded what to many businessmen was the warning that with the cessation of hostilities the spirit of the New Deal would once again be invoked. Thus the old domestic line-up of political-economic forces began to take shape. On the far right the ghosts of the isolationists stirred and the old reverie of a nineteenth-century *laissez faire*, with government no more than the mute and meek handmaiden of business, began once again to take shape. On the far left wild imaginings of a Marxist triumph fevered the minds of a small minority of men. Neither had any chance of success. But somewhere in between these extremes lay the road to the future.

Perhaps at no time in history were the American people more aware than they were in 1945 of the fact that for nearly a century the political and social institutions of their country—and their way of thinking about them—had been undergoing vast changes. America had been shifting from unrestrained private economic enterprise toward governmental intervention in commerce and industry.

As the war drew toward an end, the historian Carl Becker's question was on many lips: "How *new* will the better world be?" In this question the relationship between government and business was uppermost. Was the road ahead one that was leading us toward socialism or toward some better form of enlightened capitalism? Whichever way, the Atlantic Charter had given the clue when it referred to "improved labor standards, economic adjustment, and social security" as the economic aim of mankind.

In the prewar years the New Deal had made a brave attempt to bring about those economic ideals—full employment and full production—without which a meaningful peace and prosperity could not exist. The New Deal had accomplished something along these lines, but not enough. Perhaps its greatest achievement lay in changing the attitude of Americans toward the role of "we, the people" *versus* private enterprise. This insistence upon a fuller share in the fruits of production lay not too dormant in the minds of men during the war. The adoption of a wartime New Deal, the turning of America into the "arsenal of democracy," had shown them more than anything else the need for continuing governmental intervention in business. For the first time in history the United States had known what it meant to have the industrial plant running on full time with paying jobs for all the people.

So the dream, on every side (even on the far right), was to keep things the way they had become. Now, everyone knew, the time was fast approaching when it would be necessary to face the grave responsibilities inherent in striving for this impossible goal. In an effort to impress upon both government and the people the overwhelming necessity of not forgetting this goal, Senator Murray introduced S. 380, the so-called "full employment bill," in January, 1945. Its fundamental purpose was to establish for all time the responsibility of government for maintaining full employment through policy and action when economic failures or dislocations occurred.

Not since the early days of the New Deal had any legislative act unleashed such fundamentally opposing forces, in which the clash of economic interests, the uses of political pressure, and the mouthings of clichés came to the fore.*

The Murray bill in its own words was designed to "establish a national policy and program for assuring continuing full employment in a free competitive economy through the concerted efforts of industry, agriculture, labor, state and local governments, and the Federal government." It pronounced as national policy the duty of the federal government to foster free competitive enterprise and the investment of private capital. And it established the right to "useful, remunerative, regular and full-time employment" of all Americans who were *able and seeking to work*. Since continuing full employment was essential to protect the home, raise the standards of living, give work to returning servicemen, and to maintain national security, world peace, and expanding international trade, it placed the responsibility for achieving this goal directly on the President and the Congress.

In order to carry out these mandates the bill ordered the President to submit to Congress an annual message of economic goals, an inventory of current economic trends, and recommendations for legislation. The President was also ordered to set forth the goals necessary to achieve full employment in a National Production and Employment Budget. This document was to estimate the number of persons for whom job opportunities must be provided, the total national output necessary to create these jobs, and the total expenditures for investment by individual firms, consumers, and the government that would be required to purchase this volume of output.

Should this budget show that the prospective level of economic stability was too low to achieve a level of production that

---

* The history of this act in all its fascinating details has been told in *Congress Makes a Law,* by Stephen Kemp Bailey (New York, 1950), which traces the evolution of a single law.

would assure full employment, the President was required to suggest measures that would bring this about. These, the bill said, could be achieved through legislation on banking and currency, wages and working conditions, foreign trade and investment, agriculture, taxation, social security, and development of natural resources; or it could be achieved through encouragement of nonfederal spending by private enterprise or state and local governments, or, as a last resort, through recommendations for direct federal expenditures designed to aid the national wealth and well-being and to stimulate private enterprise, but which need not necessarily be spent for public works. In the event the economic activity was higher than necessary, the President was empowered to suggest measures to prevent "inflationary economic dislocations" and bring the required spending and investment down to the required levels.

The message and budget (which were to include measures to prevent monopolistic practices and an evaluation of the effect of recommendations on the distribution of the national income) were to be prepared in the executive offices of the President. He was to consult at all stages with the Cabinet, department heads, and advisory boards of representatives of industry, labor, agriculture, and state and local governments. Other responsibilities of the President were preparation of a quarterly review of the volume of federal investment and expenditures to ascertain if any change were warranted, and the changing of the rate of federal expenditure, when necessary to assure continuing full employment.

Once the full employment message and budget were transmitted to Congress, they were to go before a newly created joint committee of both Houses, whose membership was to be chosen so as to reflect the party strength of the Congress. This joint committee was to analyze the Presidential papers and, on or before March 1, was to report to each House a joint resolution, setting forth for the coming year specific national goals on the level of employment and economic activity and making suggestions for ways and means of achieving the bill's over-all objectives. Thus Congress would be given a presumably intelligent basis for an annual debate on economic policy, a comprehensive guide for its various committees in developing specific programs necessary to promote free enterprise and maintain continuing full employment.

Facing what they knew would be major objections to the bill, its authors built into it certain prohibitions. These forbade the government to operate plants and factories; nor did they guarantee specific jobs to specific workers. The bill did not authorize the compulsory assignment of workers to jobs. It did not guarantee individual markets or profits. It did not guarantee governmental determination of prices, wages, or output.

Public reaction to the bill was immediate and highly vocal. The National Association of Manufacturers, the United States Chamber of Commerce, the Farm Bureau Federation, and the Committee for Constitutional Government, all under the self-imposed, emergency leadership of Donaldson Brown, vice-president of General Motors and a director of the NAM, formed themselves into a tight and vocal lobby against the bill.

The businessmen of CED remained silent—at least publicly. But Ralph Flanders, recognizing that the bill in all its implications was definitely a challenge to him and his associates, called a meeting of the Research Committee to say that the field covered by the Murray bill and the high employment studies the committee had already undertaken were so similar they could not be discussed separately.

Dean Donald David, who was heading a special CED committee studying potential postwar employment, agreed that it was time "to stop, look and listen and see what has happened to the economic climate in the last two years." He pointed out that the Murray bill was not a new idea. He cited the recommendations of the Hoover Commission in 1921 and the Employment Stabilization Act, ten years later, as going as far as the Murray bill went in its statement of objectives. This, however, was an exaggeration. The Employment Stabilization Act of 1931 dealt only with public works and ignored the part played in maintaining a high level of employment through the wise use of fiscal and monetary policies by the government and by monopoly and competition. Such factors as these were, for the first time in legislative history, given full recognition in the economic picture by the Murray bill.

The bill soon became involved in intricate political maneuvering. CED's involvement in the legislative history of the Employment Act of 1946 was of significance in one way unrelated to the aims of the Act itself. It established permanently CED's position in regard to lobbying. From the beginning, as we have seen, CED purposely abided by its self-imposed rules that forbade it, as a tax-exempt educational institution, from actively seeking the passage or defeat of legislation. When Chairman Hoffman, Ralph Flanders, and Harry Scherman later testified in behalf of the bill, they did so upon the unsolicited invitation of the congressional committees involved. They carefully explained their positions. If they were appearing as representatives of CED, their prepared statements were expressions of CED policies arrived at in the sessions of the Research Committee. If they wished to "extend their remarks," as it were, to take in other ideas or suggestions, they clearly asserted that they were speaking as individuals, not as CED representatives.

The bitter opposition to the bill did not manifest itself as openly while the bill was before the Senate as it did later when it came before a conservative House committee. But the lines of opposition were drawn up early, almost as soon as its contents were made known. To those who took their stand against it, the bill was un-American because anyone who knew anything about the American way of life was well aware that a governmental guarantee of full employment was an impossible dream—a Marxist nightmare imported to bring about an end to free enterprise in a free society. The fact that the bill made no such "guarantee" did not matter to its enemies. Look at Russia, they said: Russia is a tyranny, but Russia has full employment, therefore full employment means tyranny!

Passage of the bill, its foes declared, would mean government controls over prices, investments, even the locations of industries and the mobility of the labor force. It contained an implicit threat that if free private enterprise could not supply enough jobs then the government would have to; and what did this mean if not that pretty soon the government would be providing all the employment there was? (Free enterprise sometimes seems to have very little faith in the strength of free enterprise!) Furthermore, the bill would kill individual enterprise, make people soft and dependent upon the Great White Father in Washington, and after a while they just would not work any more. Even worse it would, if passed, undermine good old Business Confidence. The government would try to maintain employment at the level of the past few abnormal years and this would bring about deficit financing and no more Balanced Budgets. Anyway, there was no possible sure method of forecasting the economic future, as the bill demanded. What would happen to America if the President should forecast a depression? It would fold up in fright. And certainly long before the government had spent enough to bring about full employment a disastrous inflation would result.

"In general," the Employment Act's historian has said, "the analysis which the conservative business pressures presented to the public and the Congress was that S.380 was totalitarian and un-American in implication, destructive of free enterprise, and dangerous and impractical in its underlying economic theories."*

But the Murray bill also had many supporters, although some

---

* In reams of pamphlets, press releases, speeches, and letters to the press and Congress, the opposition, well-financed by the NAM, the Committee for Constitutional Government, etc., said the bill would bring government controls, destruction of private enterprise, dangerously increased powers of the Executive, the legalization of socialistic federal spending and pump-priming, even if it was unworkable and impracticable. (See the many sources cited by Stephen K. Bailey in *Congress Makes a Law*. Also in Schriftgiesser, *The Lobbyists*.)

hoped for certain qualifying amendments. From President Truman down, with Secretary of the Treasury Vinson reluctantly coming to its defense at the proper time, there were many who believed it was a blow for economic freedom. If some opponents thought all the current talk about full employment was nothing but "primitive drumbeating, designed to reduce our brains to a pulp" by persons who were convinced that the "capitalistic 'free enterprise' system" was on the way out, there were others who saw vastly useful economic purposes in the bill.

They did not agree that the logic of full employment must lead to what one writer called "a closely knit network of economic controls" or that with guaranteed full employment "our liberties cannot be preserved." Instead they saw the bill as giving a chance to lodge in government a firm responsibility for maintaining, by fiscal measures, those general economic conditions in which individual enterprises can compete and prosper—the only way, perhaps, in which individual enterprise could be saved. The bill fixed responsibility for prosperous economic conditions "where it belonged"—in government. It provided adequate machinery for the discharge of this responsibility, forced the government to assemble the best possible data on current and future business trends, and made government spending only one means of combatting a depression. It was, in fact, a conservative measure. The use of the fiscal instrument, called for in the bill, was not a revolutionary change in our economic life, but one which leaves the fundamental directives and arrangements of the free enterprise system untouched.

"It recommends itself," said one economist, "because it is conservative in character. The only alternative to the indirect control of the business cycle, in which fiscal policy must be one of the instruments, is the direct control of the production and distribution machine—whether under government ownership or not."

One of the most interesting dilemmas was that faced by Eric Johnston, president of the United States Chamber of Commerce and one of the thirteen members of CED's Research Committee. Local chambers of commerce were among the most vociferous opponents of the bill, regarding it as the Communistic creation of the "Communist-sparked" CIO-PAC, and declaring it was designed to "move in Government as the new management of your company." During the Senate hearings the national Chamber of Commerce remained silent, and then when the bill came before the House took a firm stand against it. Johnston, however, refused to testify against it and although he did not publicly support it either, he joined in the unanimous position which the Research Committee was ready to place before the Senate committee when it began hearings in August.

Ralph Flanders was the first to speak on behalf of the group. "This is an epoch-making bill," the Vermonter declared, and he made clear that he was speaking not only as an individual but as a member of a group "actively concerned with accomplishing the purposes of this bill." Much of his testimony was concerned with the bill's declaration that all Americans able to work and seeking to work had a right to "useful, remunerative, regular and full-time employment."

"This right to a job is a right which I myself have come, after much thought, to accept as an objective which our society may attain." But he wanted to make it clear that, like all rights, it carried with it certain duties and responsibilities. On assuming the *right* to work, he said the individual accepted the corresponding duty to "be productive, self-reliant, and energetically in search of employment when out of a job.

"To assign the right to individuals who do not possess these qualities is to subsidize idleness and to encourage them in becoming social parasites."

Business also had a duty to operate at "its best possible efficiency" and to expand "to the limits of its capacities for solid, sustained growth." But it had no duty to furnish employment at "a continued loss." And labor had the "general responsibility" to see that wages, hours, and production standards sought by unions do not form parts of a total aggregate "which so upsets the wage-cost-price relationship as to decrease the total volume of employment." And the federal government must "do much more than store up work for release when unemployment is large. It must prevent the growth of that unemployment by policies which encourage business to expand and investors to undertake new ventures." On the basis of these duties Flanders defined the right to a job as follows:

"The man or woman out of work has the right to expect that all responsible elements of society, and particularly the government, will use all appropriate and effective means to assist his own best efforts in finding productive and profitable work."

Flanders questioned whether governmental spending could possibly provide sufficient work to break the back of a great depression but said that, if properly proportioned and properly timed, "Governmental expenditure is one of the important weapons in the arsenal for fighting unemployment." But unless the government "has done all the other things within its power to assist in maintaining stability and employment," government expenditure could not solve the problem. This could be done only by establishing a proper tax policy—by which he meant the policy defined in the CED policy statement in which the relationship between taxes and unemployment was spelled out.

Flanders supported the preparation of the National Production and Employment Budget with reservations. He was worried for fear that it would be used to effectuate policies for too long a period in advance. Furthermore he questioned the use of statistics as proposed by the Murray bill and suggested their collection be placed on a more scientific basis which would separate what he called "problem" or "residual" unemployment from the rest. He said that in order to determine what was *real* unemployment and what was *problem* unemployment, the whole field of state and federal unemployment compensation would have to be greatly widened, a proposition CED was about to make. "This extension having been made and willingness to accept a job under reasonable conditions being a prerequisite to remaining on the rolls, then we would have a definite measure not merely of the volume of unemployment, but of its location and character."

Next to appear for CED before the Senate committee was Beardsley Ruml, who devoted much of his time to a discussion of the bill's semantics. He was particularly disturbed by the use of the phrase "the right to employment."

"There has been a tendency in recent years," he said, "for those who desire a more widespread enjoyment of such benefits as education, housing, health, nutrition, and recreation to attach to these truly desirable fruits of social progress the high dignity of fundamental human rights. This extension of the term 'human right' tends to weaken the power and gravity of the concept."

He wanted all the controversial terminology of the bill—"the right to work," "the assurance of employment," and the concept "full employment"—to be modified, so that "the greatest harmony may exist among all who believe that it is both appropriate and necessary that the Federal government direct its full power toward the goal of full employment."

But as to this particular phrase, which annoyed many conservatives, he said, with typical Rumlian perspicacity:

"I like the phrase as an expression of a goal for national policy. Like other goals, it is clearly unattainable, and it would lose its virtue if it were. The statement of the goal and our sincere efforts to attain it will make the reality much closer to the ideal than if the ideal had never been expressed. There is some doubt in my mind, therefore, whether it is necessary or even desirable to define precisely what we mean by 'full employment.' It is a concept that will change from decade to decade as our ideas with respect to the relation between work and freedom change. A definition can hardly have any substantial practical consequence as to what is recommended or legislated under the bill. Why not leave the term 'full employment,' like 'liberty' and 'justice,' to stand as a goal of democratic government, and to derive its specific content from the will of the people as expressed from time to time by their free institutions?"

Then Paul Hoffman testified as Chairman of the Committee for Economic Development. He dismissed as unrealistic the viewpoint, widely held in the business community, that the bill was designed to make the federal government a permanent employer of vast masses of American workers.

"The crucial role, the most vital function of government in fostering employment, is to establish conditions under which the free enterprise system can operate most effectively and to counteract the tendencies in the system toward booms and depressions." Recognizing that government policy had become a "dominant factor in the economy," Hoffman saw the Murray bill as an instrument to develop a policy that would stimulate and stabilize free enterprise. It would make possible consideration of such tangible factors as vitalizing competition, promoting new and small business, recasting the tax structure, increasing the mobility of labor, expanding social security and unemployment benefits, and coordinating monetary and fiscal policies with particular reference to the effect on market demand.

Of "surpassing importance," he felt, were government fiscal and monetary policies. "The direct effect of the collection of taxes, of the expenditure of public funds, of the control of credit, and the indirect effect of the whole body of government fiscal and monetary policies on the confidence of businessmen and individuals exerts perhaps the greatest leverage government has on production and employment."

In the course of his testimony Hoffman asked many "billion-dollar questions," as he called them, and came to the conclusion that there were many and varied types of government action that could contribute to full employment. What was needed, more than anything else, was a penetrating and comprehensive study of them by the proper authorities. Thus he urged the immediate creation of the Joint Congressional Committee as

proposed in the Murray bill. He then suggested the creation of
what he called a "President's Commission on Full Employment."

This differed materially from the presidential setup as proposed in the bill. "This Commission," he said, abandoning the
Cabinet, agency heads, and outside advisory committees of
the bill's proposal, "should be headed by a representative of the
President. It should be a small working body composed of the
ablest men to be found. The Commission should be serviced by
a staff of the most competent authorities in the various fields. It
should make policy recommendations to the President, beginning
as promptly as possible. It should lay the groundwork for the
development of a continuing and coordinated program of
government action."

Here Hoffman was presenting the proposal that was soon to
appear in almost these same words in the CED policy statement,
Toward More Production, More Jobs and More Freedom. The
idea was discussed in the senate committee where its proponents
argued that the work on the annual economic program was so
complex it could not be done by the President alone. But it was
rejected, and the amended Murray bill went to the House. It
was a disappointment to liberals because it was too greatly
"weakened," and to conservatives because it still gave government too much "control" over private enterprise.

In the House it went before the decidedly unfriendly Committee on Expenditures headed by Rep. Carter Manasco, an Alabama
Democrat. He did his best to bury the bill in committee but was
not allowed to get away with this maneuver. Fortunately on his
committee was Rep. William Whittington of Tennessee, a conservative Southerner who took the bill seriously. Whittington at
least, unlike Manasco and Clare Hoffman, wanted to hear both
sides, and if his sentiments were those of a conservative they
were also those of a reasonable man.

In mid-October Ralph Flanders, appearing before this committee, pleaded for amendments to the original bill or acceptance
of the Senate version. He stressed the CED proposal, which by

then had been made an official CED policy by publication of the policy statement, for the Presidential commission on full employment. The bill, he said, can become "a landmark in man's long warfare against the evils of idleness and poverty."

Representative Whittington was impressed. When George Terborgh of the Machinery and Allied Products Institute proposed a somewhat similar idea, he questioned him at length. Whittington had copies of the CED policy statement and was familiar with Hoffman's August testimony. Working from all this he moved forward, seeking ideas from the U.S. Chamber of Commerce and other business sources. In his excellent history of this act Professor Bailey says that he received drafts of a substitute bill from various organizations, including CED; but, as far as CED is concerned, this is not accurate. He did, however, privately question Howard Myers and other CED staff members. After completing a vast amount of research work, Whittington drafted a substantially new bill.

Whittington's aim was to discard the last remaining remnants of what he considered dangerous federal commitments and assurances. By the board went the "Full Employment" title; out went references to "the right to employment." But the most constructive part of his revised version was a long section setting up the Council of Economic Advisors as a permanent part of the governmental machine.

Inspired to a great extent by the CED commission plan, the Council was conceived by Whittington as a realistic way to provide an acceptable economic planning mechanism in the legislative and executive branches. As such it was accepted by the House, which passed the bill on December 14, 1945. It survived the conference between Senate and the House and became the law of the land when President Truman signed the Employment Act on February 20, 1946.

Today the law is orthodoxy, even to the conservative press.

EIGHT

After Jobs—Stability

IN THE business lexicon, a shibboleth almost as popular and equally misunderstood as "Balance the Budget!" has been the cry, "Reduce the National Debt!" Even today the cry persists although a considerably different concept has guided fiscal policy for more than a decade through both Democratic and Republican administrations. And it was a group of businessmen who injected the new direction into the mainstream of national policy.

The development of the "stabilizing budget policy" has been called an outstanding intellectual achievement. Whether or not the concept merits this accolade, it has been a real contribution to economic thinking and an influence on postwar economic history.

This policy came into being because, early in their struggle with the economic facts of life, the businessmen of the Committee for Economic Development came to realize that reduction of the national debt was one—but only one—of the great objectives of a sound and workable fiscal policy. When faced with the possibility that debt reduction might not be simultaneously achievable with the maintenance of high production and employment under all circumstances, they gave priority to the latter.

This does not mean that the desirability of debt reduction was slighted. Beardsley Ruml has said it took the committee hours to write the following two sentences, but that once phrased the policy thus stated "preserved the unity of the group and was the foundation of its future work:"

"The Committee deems it wise that the tax structure and the budget should be so drawn as to make possible substantial reduction of the national debt at a high level of employment. As much debt should then be retired as is consistent with maintaining high level employment and production."

No formula was offered, however, for achieving these seemingly irreconcilable objectives. But the effort to find one went on, and in the process the "stabilizing budget policy" was devised.

The stabilizing budget policy was a sharp break from the traditional "annually balanced budget" concept. This approach to the budget meant that at times when business activity declined individual and business income also declined, thus decreasing the income of government and unbalancing the budget. When such declines occurred the federal government prevented a deficit by raising taxes or cutting expenditures, or both. But these moves also cut business and personal incomes further, and in turn reduced demand, increased unemployment, and deepened depression. At other times, when national income and therefore the revenue of government rose, the government bowed to popular demand and cut taxes or increased expenditures, or both—thus curtailing reduction of the national debt when it was most feasible to accomplish it.

Sad and recent history supported this analysis. In the prosperous twenties, when more debt reduction would have been advisable, there were tax cuts. In the depressed thirties, the annually balanced budget called for increases in taxes, taking money out of the pockets of the public at a time when there was pressing need to increase the public's demand for goods and services, and hence the level of employment.

In midsummer of 1947, Paul Hoffman told the Joint Committee of Congress on the Economic Report:

"The first major characteristic of our economy is its dynamic productiveness. The second major characteristic—and this has been its greatest weakness—is its instability."

Determined that more stability should be built into the economy, the businessmen and scholars of CED came to the conclusion that monetary, fiscal, and debt management policies were the most desirable instruments for government action. To stop a slide toward depression or a rise toward inflation, they singled out as "one essential plank in a platform for greater economic stability" a federal budget policy which should meet four tests:

It must (1) restrain demand for goods and services when inflationary conditions prevail and stimulate demand when total demand is low, prices are falling, and unemployment is high; (2) restrain unnecessary government expenditures and stimulate efficiency in government; (3) provide for the reduction of public debt under conditions of reasonable high employment; and (4) place a minimum reliance upon forecasting economic fluctuations.

This last test particularly hit directly at an alternative to the annually balanced budget which was gaining currency—the so-called "managed-compensatory" budget policy. This policy, according to CED's analysis, would attempt to fit the federal budget to the business cycle through forecasts. When employment was expected to fall below a high level, it called for tax cuts and expenditure increases in combined amounts necessary to keep the predicted decline from occurring. In the event of a predicted price boom, it called for the raising of tax rates and the cutting of expenditures to draw off buying power and to provide a surplus for debt retirement. All this, said the CED group, made sense, but—

The federal government is not geared to make the necessary changes quickly enough; and forecasting is not an accurate science. A system depending upon speed and on accurate fore-casting is inimical to stability. Under such a system, tax rates are subject to irregular and unpredictable variations that threaten business confidence.

"The really frightening possibility," the committee said, "is that we shall oscillate between adherence to the annual balance principle in prosperity and belief in compensatory spending in depression. This could only mean an endless ascent to higher and higher government spending, both in prosperity and depression."

"Since they were content," as one historian has put it, "to balance the budget over a whole trade cycle rather than every year," the CED group answered the dilemma by devising the "stabilizing budget policy." This policy was set forth in a clearly-written document called *Taxes and the Budget*, pub-lished in the fall of 1947.* It would meet four tests, the group contended, because it would set tax rates to balance the budget and provide a surplus for debt retirement at an agreed high level of employment and national income. Having set these rates, it

---

* Heading the subcommittee that produced the 73-page statement, *Taxes and the Budget*, was a newcomer to the CED board of trustees, J. Cameron Thom-son of Minneapolis, Minn., then president of the Northwest Bancorporation. In the following years Mr. Thomson has carried out many difficult assignments for CED in his role as fiscal and monetary expert and has been responsible for the preparation of most of its policy statements on these subjects. When *Taxes and the Budget* was published, there were no dissents from members of the subcommittee or from the 21-man Research and Policy committee. Other members of the subcommittee which wrote this statement were: John D. Biggers, president, Libby-Owens-Ford Glass Company; James F. Brownlee; Marion B. Folsom, then treasurer of the Eastman Kodak Company; Paul G. Hoffman; Ernest Kanzler, chairman of the board of Universal C.I.T. Credit Corporation; Raymond Rubicam; Beardsley Ruml; and Wayne C. Taylor. Technical advisors to the subcommittee were Roy Blough, then professor of economics and political science at the University of Chicago and former director of the Division of Tax Research of the U.S. Treasury; Norris Darrell, of Sullivan and Cromwell, New York; and Harry J. Rudick, of Lord, Day and Lord, and professor of law at New York University, each of whom was beginning a long association with CED. The staff work on the document was done mainly by Herbert Stein, then staff economist for CED, who became research director in 1957, following the death of Howard B. Myers, then asso-ciate director of research under Dr. Theodore O. Yntema, who is now a vice president (finance) of the Ford Motor Company and a trustee of CED.

would leave them alone unless there was some major change in national public policy or significant shifts in the level of potential productivity.

CED recognized, however, three important exceptions to this policy: (1) periodic adjustments should be made to allow for increased productivity and a growing population; (2) extraordinary and clearly nonrecurring expenditures should be handled as a phase of debt management; and (3) an economic crisis of great magnitude—severe depression or runaway inflation—would call for an emergency reduction or increase in tax rates by Congress.

The committee based its policy upon the simple and seemingly incontrovertible theory that the greatest part of federal revenues comes from the income of the taxpayers and the rate at which this income is taxed. If rates are kept constant, the federal revenue will rise as the national income rises and fall as the national income falls; but since tax rates are not changed, the lower national income would be reflected in lower federal revenues. Should the decline continue, surpluses would gradually disappear; then the budget would balance and a deficit would show up. According to this policy deficit financing during a severe depression is not regarded as sinful. A deficit created to expand government activity beyond the limits of tax revenue when business is good it regards as clearly undesirable; but a deficit prompted by an economic slump will "cushion the fall."

The stabilizing budget policy would leave tax rates unchanged unless a depression became serious and would maintain needed government expenditures to help sustain demand. It recognizes the political fact that government functions cannot be turned on or off at will nor be tailored exclusively to the object of stability. Certain expenditures (such as unemployment compensation) are bound to go up, but they help maintain total demand.

Assisted by such programs as unemployment compensation, the stabilizing budget policy would help to lessen the wide fluctuations of the business cycle. The ups and downs of the economy itself would determine its action, not in response to predictions, nor after events had been reduced to statistics, but almost as soon as they happened. Once set up, this policy would not call for frequent changes in order to be effective.

But there were certain prerequisites: high employment must be defined (CED set it at 96 per cent of the labor force); the price level and national income figure at which we would have high employment must be determined; and tax rates must be adjusted to and provide a desired surplus at high level employment (CED set it at 3 billion dollars of tax revenue in excess of federal expenditures).

The committee raised a question of considerable significance when it asked which of the two federal budgets should be balanced, the administrative control budget or the consolidated cash budget. When budgets were small it made little difference which was referred to, but with the development in 1937 of social security (and since then of other government corporations handling large sums of money), it became necessary to distinguish between them.

The administrative control budget, as its name implies, is designed for administrative and financial control. It shows transactions between government agencies, but it excludes certain transactions between the government and the people, and where convenient it carries some items on an accrual basis. As an instrument of administrative control it is indispensable.

The consolidated cash budget serves a different and more inclusive purpose, which is basically to measure the impact of government transactions on the economy. It does this because, being "consolidated," it includes *all* transactions between the government and the people, and it excludes all transfers between the internal agencies of the federal government itself. Furthermore, it is also a cash budget, because it shows in the intake and outgo on a cash basis in the year in which the transaction actually takes place.

Sometimes, as it did in fiscal 1947, the consolidated cash budget will reveal a greater surplus than the administrative budget and sometimes, as in 1951, it will reveal a smaller surplus. In either event it shows more clearly the state of the economy, for it reveals a budget that is balanced (or unbalanced) in the economic, rather than the bookkeeping sense. But in the latter sense it is the cash consolidated budget that should be balanced; for balancing the administrative budget is meaningless in that, being an administrative budget, it can be balanced at any time by the mere devices of definition, inclusions, or exclusions. It was CED's belief that the adoption of the cash-consolidated budget introduced economic criteria rather than fisco-administrative criteria into federal fiscal policy as a test of sound fiscal planning.

Summed up, CED's tax policy, as rigorously established in this 1947 statement and as adhered to with minor exceptions for the next ten years as the formula for its statements on national fiscal policy, was as follows:

Tax rates should be set high enough to balance the budget or yield a modest surplus at high employment and national income. Neither for the purpose of offsetting variations in revenues and expenditures resulting from deviations in national employment or income, nor for countering actual or predicted moderate fluctuations, should this basic principle be disturbed. Only when serious unemployment or inflation is encountered or *confidently* predicted should larger deficits, or surpluses, be sought.

High employment, which is the crux of the policy, is employment at 96 per cent of the labor force. The moderate surplus was originally defined as 3 billion dollars, but this was set at zero in 1954. Large nonrecurring expenditure need not immediately be covered by taxes. Tax reductions, made possible by gradual growth of the tax base, should be made at intervals to avoid the unsettling effect of annual revisions.

In calculating the high employment level of the national income, the CED formula uses, in general, the existing price level. Inflations or recessions of less than disastrous magnitude call for no departure from the basic rule about the tax rate, although such fluctuations may justify short adjustments in the timing of tax actions. Tax reductions that are justified by the basic rule but are too small to accommodate a balanced program may be deferred. In any case, before taxes can be cut, *assurance* rather than mere probability that a deficit will be avoided must be the rule.

The idea of using fiscal reform to discourage either inflation or unemployment was set forth none too soon. Within the next eighteen months the nation was to experience dangerous doses of both.

The annual Economic Report to the Congress, called for by the Employment Act, which President Truman sent to Congress in January, 1948, painted an ominous picture of inflationary trends. All through the report ran the warning that prices and wages both were moving up so rapidly that in spite of his past warnings to business and labor, Mr. Truman said, at "the end of the year there was a continuing prospect of a fruitless and dangerous spiraling of prices and wages."

"The record of prices, wages and profits"—these last were substantially above the 1946 level—"shows how they fed upon one another in a developing process of inflation. In spite of the heartening production record of the year, this inflationary trend was profoundly disturbing. It not only produced great inequities among our people, but also created the danger of a serious set-back.

"The purposes of the Employment Act are beginning to meet their first real test. Unless we as a nation show an ability to impose restraints upon ourselves and to utilize the machinery of our representative government to devise well-considered regula tory measures, we stand in great danger that runaway prices, overextended credit, and unbalanced developments will lead to an economic recession. We cannot be sure that such a recession would not be severe and recovery slow and painful.

"The first objective for 1948 must be to halt the inflationary trend."

Yet, within less than a year, unemployment began to displace inflation as the major worry. In January, 1949, alone, 700,000 persons were laid off. Unemployment, at 2,650,000, had reached a postwar peak. General Motors cut its automobile prices while workers on the slowed-down assembly lines took an automatic cut in wages in accordance with the cost-of-living clauses in their contracts. By July, unemployment had reached 6 per cent of the civilian labor force (seasonally adjusted) and by the twentieth anniversary of the Great Crash of October, 1929, the jobless had risen to 7 per cent of the labor force.

Although most economic advisors called the signs merely "disinflation," there were others who saw in them indications that perhaps the United States was on the edge of a real recession. Whether goaded by rising prices or rising unemployment, the search for stability went on. The result was two major engagements on the economic battlefront: one around credit and the other around controls. And the persistent pursuit of economic research led the trustees of CED straight into important roles in both of these battles.

The first arose from a situation that had existed for several years and was by now becoming so acute as to be generally recognized as a feud between the Treasury Department and the supposedly independent Federal Reserve System. A major point in Treasury policy had been to maintain the interest on the federal debt at as low a point as possible. This policy demanded close cooperation by the central bank, which was forced to provide an "easy" supply of money. In order to do this the Federal Reserve was forced to "surrender" much of its legal power to "tighten the money market" at times when it felt the inflationary trend made such action necessary.

During the war, of course, an "easy" money market, which allowed the government to borrow needed funds, was a necessity as long as the Treasury had to borrow from the banks. But by the end of 1948 an important and vocal segment of public opinion, of which CED was an outspoken part, was demanding that the Federal Reserve reassert its independence from the administration's "control."

In further development of the "stabilizing budget policy," CED's research group issued a policy statement which plunged it directly into the heart of this controversy. *Monetary and Fiscal Policy for Greater Economic Stability*, issued in December, 1948, was posited on the grounds that these aspects of national policy "encourage or discourage economic expansion or contraction without prescribing the channels through which economic enterprise shall flow." The statement warned that monetary and fiscal policies alone could not achieve the goal of stabilization. Wage and price policies and the structure of markets for labor and goods, agricultural policy, foreign trade and international finance, the construction industry, savings-investment institutions, and business policies were among the other economic problems that must also be studied to develop a full program for economic stability.

The report divided its recommendations into two parts, one dealing with periods of inflation, the other with periods of depression. During inflationary periods it said the following measures would "contribute to stability by restraining the rise of total expenditure":

1. Hold tax rates stable, so that revenues will rise as the national income rises and the government surplus will increase.

2. Tighten the reserve position of the banks, by Federal Reserve sales of government securities in the open market, by increase of rediscount rates and/or by increase of reserve requirements.

3. Use the government surplus to retire debt held by the commercial banking system, including the Federal Reserve banks.

4. Refund maturing government debt in a way that will reduce the holdings of the banking system.

5. Reduce the volume of government loans and guarantees of loans.

In periods of depression the CED report called for a reversed course:

1. Hold tax rates stable, so that tax revenues will fall as the national income falls and the government surplus will decline or fall into a deficit. In extreme conditions a temporary reduction of tax rates may be desirable to stimulate private expenditure.

2. Expand the money supply by open-market purchase of government securities; further ease the reserve position of the banks by reduction of rediscount rates and/or by reduction of reserve requirements.

3. Finance a deficit by borrowing in a way that will induce the commercial banking system to acquire government securities, with such Federal Reserve action in providing additional bank reserves as may be necessary for this purpose.

4. Refinance maturing federal debt in part by borrowing from the commercial banking system, including the Federal Reserve banks.

5. Expand the volume of federal loans and guarantees of loans within the scope of the federal-loan program accepted as appropriate in the long run.

These recommendations led directly into the question between the Treasury and the Federal Reserve—a question that, incidentally, was basically, although in modern form, the age-old one of creditors versus debtors that has been with us since the days when Alexander Hamilton and Albert Gallatin were thrashing it out in the early sessions of our Congress.

CED stated that "in its decisions as to the purchase and sale of government bonds, the Federal Reserve should act on the basis of its judgment from time to time as to the effect of such action *on the economy as a whole*." At that time the market for government bonds was pegged at par. The CED was concerned (and, of course, was not alone in this) lest in its open-market operations the Federal Reserve should be coerced by the Treasury and other agencies of government "to act too narrowly in the meeting of specific difficulties and in the solution of specific problems."

The Federal Reserve also should "give due consideration to requirements arising out of unsettled international relations," the statement continued. "However, the Federal Reserve should feel free to reduce the support level unless it finds a superior alternative way of bringing about a monetary restriction, when and if that is required by the objective of economic stability."

As to the Treasury Department, it should, when deciding on the character of its continuous refinancing, give "great weight to the effects of different kinds of borrowing on the general inflationary or deflationary situation." In time of inflation the Treasury should borrow in ways that do not add to the money supply and that would be least likely to draw idle funds into use. In time of depression the Treasury should borrow in ways that "exercise the least restraint upon private expenditure, essentially by borrowing from the banking system."

Furthermore it suggested that Congress should pay attention to the question of whether its programs for government lending were "of a character that will contribute to the solution of the stabilization program." In order to coordinate the activities of the many government lending and loan guarantee agencies, it proposed the creation of a Federal Loan Council, which would review all lending and loan guarantee policies in order to make them consistent with an over-all federal stabilization program.

In thus distinctly drawing the issues between the Treasury and the Federal Reserve and making clear recommendations concerning them, the report played an important role in the famous 1951 "accord" which was to restore the Federal Reserve to a position where it could independently act to put the brakes on when it was convinced that inflation threatened to get out of control.

It was fear of recession, however, that set the stage for the next big battle.

Since 1947 the Economic Reports of the President had contained several strong intimations that, in order to keep the economy on an even keel, some administrative controls might have to be resorted to. President Truman had asked for control powers when he had gone to Congress late in 1947 to ask for emergency aid to France, Italy, and Austria as a prelude to the European Recovery Program. But the Eightieth Congress had refused them, although it had sanctioned certain voluntary allocation agreements and had extended then existing transportation and export controls.

As spending for defense reached new heights in the spring of 1948, the administration again renewed its pleas for such powers. In passing the Selective Service Act in June, Congress empowered the President to require precedence for defense contracts and it placed a priority on steel needed for defense. Thus, in the name of defense, the postwar wall against governmental controls over the economy was breached. A month later President Truman asked for extended economic powers. These included an excess profits tax, the restoration of consumer credit controls, greater control by the Federal Reserve of bank credit, control of speculation in the commodity markets, and the extension of rent control. He also asked for "stand-by authority" to ration products in short supply that "vitally affect the health and welfare of the people," and for control of prices of scarce commodities that "basically affect essential production or the cost of living." He said at that time that, on the basis of present facts, he did not think he would have to use them.

Congress reluctantly restored consumer credit controls and allowed the Federal Reserve to increase reserve requirements to member banks, but it refrained from granting price controls and allocation authority. This, of course, did not satisfy President Truman, and, in January, 1949, he once again asked for control and allocation powers to be used on a "selective basis" where needed to combat either recession or inflation. The latter was most on his mind. "We are still in a situation where the prices of certain critical materials and commodities are moving upward for the third consecutive year," he said. "Sharp rises in the price of essential products may be harmful to the economy even where the general price level is fairly stable. Further, we cannot be certain that another upsurge of general inflation will not reappear this year under the composite pressures that are at work throughout the economy."

The following month a bill that would have created an "Economic Stability Act" was introduced in Congress. This would permanently have given the President the power to control prices and allocate commodities. Introduced by Rep. Brent Spence of Kentucky, but generally believed to have been the brain child of Leon Keyserling and John D. Clark, economic advisors to the President, it set off a bitter debate that raged through the winter and spring.

The Spence bill raised the hackles of all private enterprisers, not only because of the powers of allocation and price control it would confer on the President, but also because it would give him wide discretionary power to undertake the construction of new productive capacity in areas where he deemed shortages to exist and where private industry was unwilling to undertake the expansion considered necessary. Screams of "Socialism!" and worse poured from many segments of the business community throughout the land.

In their reactions, the businessmen and educators of CED concentrated on *The Uses and Dangers of Direct Controls in Peacetime*, which was the title of the policy statement they issued in July, 1949. While recognizing that governmental intervention in the economy under certain situations was not only warranted but desirable, the statement was sharp and incisive in its criticism of peacetime controls. Its basic theory was that controls would undermine our economic and political institutions by increasing the power of the Executive at the expense of the legislature and that, by substituting administrative decisions for the automatic operation of the price system, they would deprive the country of the advantage of a market economy.

"We would be on weak ground in making these objections,"

the statement said, "if our attitude was merely one of opposition and if we held that the proper function of government is to do nothing." As it had asserted vigorously in three previous policy statements* the committee now clung to its belief that the survival of our social and economic systems *requires positive governmental action at proper times* if stability is to be achieved. But it was equally convinced that—except in times of war or the imminence of war—this objective could, and should, be approached through fiscal and monetary policies.

One of the most significant aspects of this statement was its expression of a fundamental philosophy by a consequential group of businessmen concerning the relationship of the business community to society and the government. It revealed an inherent liberalism in its approach to the changed political and economic conditions that had begun with Theodore Roosevelt's New Nationalism, had been extended by Woodrow Wilson's New Freedom, and most of all by Franklin D. Roosevelt's New Deal. Out of these three great liberal movements, each in its way anti-business, had emerged a new conception of what Arthur M. Schlesinger, Jr. has called "a social welfare state in which the national government had the express obligation to maintain high levels of employment in the economy, to supervise standards of life and labor, to regulate the methods of business competition, and to establish comprehensive standards of social security." This new conception CED understood and accepted, but it also put limits upon it in no uncertain terms.

Expanding the power of administrative agencies—except those set up to control public utilities and transportation, industries whose inherent nature made such agencies necessary—was opposed because it felt it was impossible for Congress to legislate the *details* of a price-control or allocation system. If Congress tried to do so, the price system would be deprived of what little

* *Taxes and the Budget*, 1947; *Monetary and Fiscal Policy for Greater Economic Stability*, 1948; and, in May, 1949, *Tax and Expenditure Policy for 1949.*

capacity for flexible adjustment it would retain under administrative control. Discretionary power to impose limitations on what can be produced or consumed, or even on incomes people can earn, should not be placed in the hands of administrators in a democratic state.

The granting of such administrative powers opens the door to strong pressures to use them for purposes other than those originally intended by the legislature. An "attempt to legislate through the administrative process is the surest road to minority rule." In 1949, it should be remembered, lobbying by minority economic and other pressure groups in Washington was reaching such proportions that, in spite of the Lobby Act of 1946, a select committee of the House of Representatives was about to launch an investigation which, it was vainly hoped, would include a study of the power of pressure groups on administrative agencies.

Not only do direct controls tend to create the shortages they are supposed to avoid, CED said, but they are antagonistic to the economic growth of the nation. Private enterprise thrives on its search for new techniques and new products and this calls for risk-taking investment. The "bureaucratic process" of price adjustment freezes the pattern of allocation so firmly that new firms cannot break in and the enterprising firm cannot grow. To the ordinary investment risk is added the hazard of having to guess the forthcoming decisions of a government agency.

Although CED admitted that, for a limited period and under such circumstances as a war, a system of controls can work, it pointed out that it does so only on the basis of prices previously established in the market. The longer such a system is continued the more arbitrary it becomes. The yardstick for controls must be based on the past rather than on the future, thus preventing the progress, change, and economic growth, "so vital to a dynamic economy."

The committee found it was delusion to think that prices of some commodities could be held down by controls in an inflationary period while others were permitted to rise. It dismissed controls entirely as a means to fight inflation. For that purpose the best system, indeed the *only* system, was the judicious use of fiscal and monetary policy.

"The fiscal and monetary approach has the great advantage," it optimistically declared, "of establishing control over the *total* flow of purchasing power and leaving the price mechanism unimpaired. Within a stable framework achieved by such measures, the price and wage adjustments needed to increase production, to encourage technological advance, and to achieve an appropriate allocation of resources, can be made."

In July, the same month in which this policy statement was issued, President Truman dropped his demands for controls to fight inflation. In his midyear Economic Report he admitted that the United States was in the midst of a recession. But he felt, upon examining the figures, that "on balance" the recuperative tendencies outweighed those that were causing alarm. The 1948 tax cut, which had been passed over his veto, was beginning to show its effect upon the economy.

In fact, things were so much better by mid-July that President Truman, who was taking an increasingly conservative attitude toward business, dropped his fight for stringent controls over the economy. The mischievous Spence bill withered on the vine, and the search for stability shifted to other grounds, grounds which less than a year later would erupt under the impact of the Communist attack in North Korea and a semiwar economy at home.

NINE

Economic Policy Goes International

AT ONE of the first meetings of the businessmen assembled under Secretary Jesse Jones's watchful eye in the spring of 1942, it was agreed that "the importance of foreign trade" should be of fundamental interest. And in his letter accepting the chairman-ship of the group, Paul Hoffman laid down the relating "of international lending" to the "purpose of creating maximum employment in the United States" as a major field of research. This emphasis was to create a document of historic importance, help establish two major international financial institutions, and ultimately put Hoffman at the helm of what Senator Arthur H. Vandenberg called "the turning point in history for 100 years to come."

During these same months of 1942, the realization began to grow in both the United States and Great Britain that some kind of international machinery needed to be created to provide financial credits for postwar reconstruction and resource de-velopments. In the United States Treasury Department, Harry Dexter White, then unsuspected of Communist leanings, was putting his brilliant mind to work on the problem. In England, Lord Keynes, then but four years from the end of his amazing career, was similarly engaged.

The need stimulating the independent studies of these two brilliant men was noted at one of the first sessions of the scholars brought together to form the Research Advisory Board of the Committee for Economic Development. Robert D. Calkins, now the president of the Brookings Institution, suggested the creation of a conference of international monetary experts—and this was fully a year before President Roosevelt's invitation brought the representatives of forty-one nations to meet amidst the picturesque mountains of Bretton Woods, New Hampshire, in the summer of 1944.

Thomas W. Lamont of J. P. Morgan Company, reacting to the suggestions of CED's scholars, prophetically declared:

"We do have the opportunity to make a real presentation of the problem. Keynes and White are busy promoting mechanisms and neglecting the problems."

The attack on the problems by CED began with the commissioning of Professor Calvin B. Hoover of Duke University to prepare a research study on the broad general subject of "International Problems After the War." Dr. Jacob Viner of Princeton, Dr. John Henry Williams of Harvard University, Dr. Arthur Upgren of Dartmouth, and several others were engaged to assist him.

Hoover began hesitantly. He feared that what he called his "heterodox views on international trade, which flowed from a general point of view as a Keynesian," might be unacceptable to a group of businessmen. Furthermore, he told the trustees of CED at his first meeting with them, "I am greatly afraid of depressions and inject this thinking into all my analyses. I feel very strongly that continuing positive measures must be taken to prevent unemployment and to achieve something like full employment. I think, too, that all economists are basically and almost instinctively free traders."

He failed to frighten the businessmen and he began his study for them in the spring of 1943. His work was interrupted by a trip on government business to England and Sweden where he talked with scholars like Gunnar Myrdal and with scores of industrialists. But in January, 1944, he was ready to present his draft report. The fifty people who gathered to hear him included not only CED trustees and their academic advisers but also the president of the National Association of Manufacturers, a representative of the American Federation of Labor, the editor of *Fortune*, and a visiting British industrialist.

For six hours Calvin Hoover was subjected to severe cross-examination on almost every conceivable aspect of "international problems after the war": the repayment of Lend-Lease, the future of the merchant marine, government subsidies, synthetic rubber, aluminum, and magnesium, the gold policy, the use of agricultural surpluses, cartels, export and import balances and imbalances, reciprocal trade agreements, tariffs, and so on, until, when asked why he had not touched upon still another subject, he sighed, "I'd like to, but I've already got more hay down than I can get in the barn."

Finally, toward the end of one of the most rigorous sessions of what Beardsley Ruml has called "that hard-working and stubborn crowd," they came to Keynes and White and their plans. There was much skepticism expressed about the proposed international fund, especially by Sumner Slichter, who at that time felt there was much "specious reasoning being put forward regarding the flexibility that such plans provide." And Ralph Flanders—who today considers the role CED played in ratifying the plans among its outstanding contributions—doubted "that any of these schemes contribute anything really fundamental. Recent proposals for an international bank for reconstruction tie more directly into the problem of employment than do the Keynes and White plans," he said prophetically. But Hoover felt that something workable could be evolved from both and that the obstacles could be overcome.

"It would be well," Ralph Flanders once told a research committee meeting, "if we could preserve the wisdom not to proceed disastrously towards desirable ends."

The Bretton Woods Conference, however, almost managed to proceed in that very manner. Its primary purpose was to establish the International Monetary Fund in an attempt to bring some order into the jungle of international currency principles—the source from which a dollar-hungry world would satisfy its requirements. The World Bank, which emerged from the conference and today plays a far more prominent role, was an afterthought. It came close to being the disaster that blocked achievement of the desirable end.

Harry Dexter White and Lord Keynes directed the two commissions which did the greater part of the work of the conference, which was attended by 400 delegates and presided over by Secretary of the Treasury Henry Morgenthau, Jr. Out of their labors came a far-reaching agreement. The International Monetary Fund—at the start set at 8,800 million dollars to be contributed by member nations according to fixed quotas—was created primarily to see that the currencies of the world were exchanged at a nearly constant rate. It was also devised to cushion members against temporary dislocations in foreign trade. When such shocks occurred, the nations could buy from the Fund such foreign currencies as they needed, paying in their own money. Each nation agreed not to alter the par value of its currency except after consulting with the Fund and in harmony with certain basic rules.

The International Bank for Reconstruction and Development (World Bank) was to be given a potential capital of 10 billion dollars, to be used for making loans to member nations for projects which private banking sources would not support, however badly needed, and which an expert investigation proved to be economically sound. At the end of the devastating war, with many nations impoverished, these monies, which ordinary banks could not supply, could serve a useful purpose in supplying the wherewithal to rebuild devastated cities, ports, and industries.

Since the United States was the most heavily industrialized of all nations, and since it held nearly 20 billion dollars, or more than half of all the world's gold, its contribution was necessarily large: $2,750,600 to the Fund, $1,200,000 to the Bank. In spite of this huge commitment, which caused some uneasiness in the breasts of latent isolationists, the idea of both the Fund and the Bank struck the popular imagination.

Persons who knew nothing of foreign exchange, international banking, or even foreign trade were moved by what seemed to be a potentiality for good in the postwar world. Perhaps the mere fact that American bankers were as a whole against the Bretton Woods proposals brought an emotional support to the idea that it would otherwise not have had, for the American people traditionally have never quite trusted the banking fraternity. At any rate, in liberal circles there was a profound belief that the Bretton Woods proposals were on the side of international decency. They became a part of the bright air of expectation that hung over America in the last year of the war. In many minds Bretton Woods was linked with Dumbarton Oaks: strange but meaningful phrases which—somehow—meant much to the hope of the free new world that was to come when the dictators were defeated and democracy had won.

But as soon as the Bretton Woods proposals were made public bitter controversy arose. This centered around the question of whether the International Monetary Fund should be set up, or whether its functions could not better be performed by the proposed World Bank, which would give these functions the same scrutiny that the Bank was expected to bring to bear on the making of loans for reconstruction or development.

The bankers, well-organized and led by the American Bankers Association, were almost unanimously convinced that the Fund, since it involved the exchange of currencies as a matter of right, would be subject to abuses which, they said, would result in the unbalancing of its accounts and the freezing of its resources as soon as its hard currencies, especially dollars, were exhausted.

The administration, led by Secretary Morgenthau, and seemingly with the backing of the general public, insisted that the proposals be adopted as they stood. It argued that any change or modification, such as placing the Monetary Fund under the supervision of the World Bank, would defeat the purpose of the Fund and perhaps preclude any international agreement for a workable financial program after the war. If the United States accepted the proposals only after major revisions were made, these would have to be thrown back to another international conference for approval. The administration knew that this would be almost impossible to bring about.

Debate continued on this issue between the administration and the bankers, whose appointed committees drew up reports and analyses to meet the administration's arguments. None of the large business organizations came to the defense of the proposals. Silence from the National Association of Manufacturers and the United States Chamber of Commerce was as effective as action would have been. Grimly the administration stood its ground for whole hog or none. A deadlock, if not rejection, seemed imminent.

At the crucial moment in the sometimes violent public controversy, the businessmen of the Committee for Economic Development intervened. It was, as Beardsley Ruml later testified, a triumph for the process of business-academic research; all the more so because "in spite of all the rush and pressure, the procedures of the Research Committee with respect to meetings, footnote privileges and the rest were respected in meticulous detail."

It is not without irony that this organization of businessmen should have been the first and most effective outside agency to come to the solid defense of what the *London Observer* once described as a "characteristically Rooseveltian institution: that is a fascinatingly ambivalent blend of the revolutionary and the conventional, bold but tentative in conception, a little vague, a little self-contradictory even, but also flexible and capable of organic growth."

The Bretton Woods proposals were first discussed seriously in

CED at a meeting held late in December, 1944. Less than a month later (January 21, 1945) another Research Committee meeting was called. Between the two sessions word had spread throughout official Washington that CED was studying the differences between the proponents and opponents of what President Roosevelt, in his message to Congress, had called "the cornerstone for international cooperation." The second meeting was significant, for among those who were invited to sit down with the full membership of the Research Committee and the Research Advisory Board and Dr. Yntema's staff were Harry Dexter White, Assistant Secretary of the Treasury, Herbert Feis, special consultant to the Secretary of War, and L. D. Stinebower, representing the State Department. All took part in the fervent discussion. White, who represented the official administration viewpoint, was especially persuasive in his plea that CED support the proposals as they stood.

"A report of this group," he said, "would be most influential. I would like to make a plea that your forthcoming policy statement cover the immediate issues, on which your weight can be felt. The other things can be presented in another document."

At the conclusion of the meeting White's suggestion was adopted, but with a difference, and perhaps less because of his arguments than because Paul Hoffman, Ralph Flanders, Beardsley Ruml, Calvin B. Hoover, and R. Gordon Wasson (vice-president of J. P. Morgan and Company and successor to Thomas Lamont on the Research Committee) were impressed by the immediacy of the issue—and because they felt they had found a solution to the dilemma facing Congress and the bankers.

The solution was a simple one. The bankers had contended that the Fund would become unbalanced and frozen because countries would improperly use their privilege of exchanging currencies and that temporary imbalances would be the beginning of what in the end would become stabilization loans. For this reason they wanted the World Bank's management to take over the function of the currency exchange. The administration, on the other hand, held that any country rightfully should have the privilege to exchange its currency through the Fund in order to correct temporary shortages, and that such transactions were not loans and should not be examined as such.

Although everyone else called it a compromise, CED preferred to call its solution a "synthesis" of the opposing factions. It recommended that the World Bank be given the power to make both long-term and short-term stabilization loans, when these loans could be justified and when they served to meet requirements lying outside the purposes of the Fund. It pointed out that the charter of the proposed World Bank stated that the Bank was to be authorized to make loans for reconstruction, development, and "other purposes." All that had to be done was to make it clear, in the wording of the charter, that this phrase "other purposes" *did include* stabilization loans. Thus would the position of the Bank be protected and the danger to the Fund be removed, for then the managers of the Fund could refer all inappropriate transactions to the Bank.

It was Harry Scherman who most clearly showed why the proposition was really a synthesis and not, as the press generalized, a compromise. In testimony before the House Banking and Currency Committee in April he said:

"By giving the Bank managers the *express* power to make stabilization loans, and by not making them *assume* that power by interpretation . . . is not to broaden the Bank's power, but to make sharper and clearer to all the nations concerned what are the separate functions and responsibilities of the Bank and Fund."

As Scherman told the committee, the suggestion was acceptable to the Treasury as "constructive and clarifying." It had been approved in a public address by Secretary Vinson. It therefore appeared, he said, "as if at least one-half of the synthesis of opposing views may have been effectuated." What of the other half? "Well," he said, "it seems not to have been observed that this idea is that of the American Bankers Association itself!"

He then pointed out that three of the opposing suggestions of the ABA were pertinent only if the Monetary Fund were to be discarded. The fourth read: "That the lending powers of the Bank be broadened . . . to allow it to make loans, *under the same safeguards as the other loans of the Bank,* for the purpose of aiding countries in stabilizing currencies.

"Here, therefore, in the most important recommendation of the American Bankers Association—together with the approval given the CED suggestion by the Treasury—is evidence of the complete synthesis effectuated between the opposing views. They do not compromise on this basic point, because neither is changing its viewpoint. They agree. The ABA says that the Bank ought to have the power to make stabilization loans. The Treasury agrees with CED that it is well to have this power expressly granted."

The Bretton Woods Proposals: A Statement on National Policy, with a cogent foreword by Ralph Flanders, was made public on March 19. "Within forty-eight hours both the government and the bankers agreed that the CED proposal left very little in dispute," Ruml has said. The compromise, or "synthesis," was the answer all had been waiting for. It cut further debate. Later Flanders as well as Scherman appeared before committees of both Houses, upon invitation, to testify in clarification of the CED statement. The House amended the bill according to the CED suggestion, as later did the Senate. Late in June President Truman, who had believed with President Roosevelt that the Bank and the Fund were essential to international economic postwar cooperation, singled out CED for praise for its singular part in saving the Bretton Woods proposals from disaster. On July 19 the Senate ratified the agreement by a vote of 61 to 16, while President Truman was conferring with Stalin and Churchill at Potsdam.

CED's role in this historic affair was further justification of the CED system of objective research on questions of public policy and proof that its unique methods could be directed toward resolving a controversy even after it had descended from the higher realms of international economics to the lower levels of domestic politics.

This experience in resolving international economics with domestic politics was soon to play a decisive role in what is still probably the most significant foreign policy decision of the post-war period—the European Recovery Program.

Both the foreign economic and the domestic political front were scenes of increasing chaos through 1946 and 1947. Strikes that stretched all the way from the workers in major industries, over wages, to the buyers in remote villages, over prices, gave evidence of the turmoil at home. The battered Truman administration waged uncertain battle with a Republican majority in Congress that was aroused by the scent of victory and was struggling internally for the power that its leaders were certain would become theirs in 1948.

Only in foreign policy was there a measure of cooperation—thanks largely to the statesmanship of Senator Arthur H. Vandenberg who worked closely with the administration in the formation of the United Nations, the frustrating efforts of the Council of Foreign Ministers to conclude peace treaties, and in assessing the impact of the growing rift of the United States with its ally, the Soviet Union.

This bipartisanship did not, however, extend to foreign economic policy. Relief, rehabilitation, and restoration of trade were the administration's major preoccupations, but only on relief could it expect cooperation from the Republican Congress. In the Senate, even relief had to pass under the searching scrutiny of Majority Leader Robert A. Taft, whose isolationist sentiments were bolstered by his desire to fulfill his party's tax-cut promises. And in the House, Majority Leader Everett M. Dirksen was willing to support emergency food and medical relief but balked at a program for rehabilitation. On trade, the Republican majority was determined to limit the administration's powers to cut rates under the reciprocal trade agreements and kept nipping at the heels of Undersecretary of State for Economic Affairs Will Clayton with a running investigation of the whole trade program.

In Europe, the harshest winter in living memory on top of the war's destruction had brought the Western democratic regimes to the verge of disaster by the spring of 1947. Britain, facing economic collapse at home, was fighting a rear-guard action by abandoning its commitments overseas. The question of whether the vacuum left by Britain's withdrawal would be filled by the United States or the Soviet Union posed an issue which even our divided government could not avoid. Nevertheless, the relatively modest Greek-Turkish Aid bill had a stormy passage through the Congress, even with the aid of the strong Stop Communism tide. And the Republican congressional leadership retaliated by slashing away a few weeks later at the administration's appropriation for emergency relief.

It was in the midst of this political storm that Secretary of State George C. Marshall modestly but courageously launched his trial balloon at the Harvard Commencement of June 5, 1947. While the Europeans responded with hopeful speed, the dust of the political storm here at home rose higher, and by November *Business Week* magazine was warning:

"Business would do well to convince Congress that Marshall Plan aid is a matter of industrial health, not of politics. Industry in this country cannot long prosper with the non-Communist world suffering postwar paralysis."

Some businessmen were beginning to respond. Shortly after Secretary Marshall's Harvard speech, President Truman responded to a suggestion made by Senator Vandenberg and appointed nineteen "distinguished citizens" to a "President's Committee on Foreign Aid." Nine were businessmen and five of these nine, including Paul Hoffman, were trustees of CED.* The six academic representatives included Calvin B. Hoover and

* Hiland Batchellor, president, Allegheny-Ludlum Steel Corporation; John L. Collyer, President, B. F. Goodrich Company; Chester C. Davis, president,

Edward S. Mason of CED's Research Advisory Board, and the executive secretary was Richard M. Bissell, Jr., who had been close to CED ever since he had helped draw up the original plans for it as an aide to Jesse Jones.

The Harriman Committee, as it became known through the chairmanship of Secretary of Commerce Averill Harriman, worked at full speed throughout the summer and into the autumn. At the beginning there was some disagreement as to whether the programs should be envisaged as essentially a charity or as a cooperative effort to bring about economic recovery. The complete commitment of the businessmen from CED to productivity as the key to economic progress and political stability was a powerful influence in reaching the decision to emphasize recovery.

Although the amount and duration of the aid to be given posed issues almost as fundamental, these proved to be easier to resolve than some of the subsidiary questions. One of the thorniest disagreements arose over using the aid program to foster expansion of free enterprise in countries with socialist governments. Critics of the aid program claimed that it would be used to coddle socialism. The existence of a socialist government in Britain and the possibility of other socialist governments on the Continent made this a major issue for some. Certain members of the committee believed it was important to meet this issue squarely, especially since they were convinced that expansion of free enterprise would speed recovery. Others, including Chairman Harriman, were opposed to shaping the program for this specific purpose.

Paul Hoffman became the mediator between these points of view and the position finally agreed upon was embodied in this balanced, temperate statement:

"Aid from this country should not be conditioned on the methods used to reach these (agreed) goals, so long as they are

Federal Reserve Bank of St. Louis; and R. R. Deupree, president, Procter and Gamble Company.

consistent with basic democratic principles. Continued adherence to such principles is an essential condition to continued
aid, but this condition should not require adherence to any form
of economic organization or the abandonment of plans adopted
and carried out in a free and democratic way. While this committee firmly believes that the American system of free enterprise is the best method of obtaining high productivity, it does
not believe that any foreign-aid program should be used as a
means of requiring other countries to adopt it."

The persistence of this issue and its ability to influence attitudes toward the entire program was recognized in the CED
Policy Statement which was issued three months after the release
of the Harriman Committee report, and which declared:

"We believe that free enterprise with its incentives and its
encouragement of individual initiative is the best method for
achieving [expansion of production]. However, we also believe
that each country must be left free to decide on its own methods
of organizing production."

In his work on this issue and others that had arisen in the
Harriman Committee, Hoffman and his CED colleagues received
support from the research group which had been set up within
CED itself.

The previous year, Ralph Flanders had resigned his chairmanship of the Research and Policy Committee to enter the United
States Senate—an event reported by *Business Week* under the
headline "Vermont Gives CED Man to the Senate." He had
been succeeded by Raymond Rubicam, who had organized the
advertising firm of Young and Rubicam at the age of thirty-one
and was so successful that in 1944 at the age of fifty he retired
to spend more time on work that "involved the study of political
economy." He had the respect for research that was beginning
to gain a foothold in the business world; in fact he had pioneered
in the introduction of scientific method into advertising by
persuading a young professor at Northwestern University named
George H. Gallup to become the head of his marketing research.

Together Hoffman and Rubicam persuaded Wayne Chatfield Taylor to head a CED research and policy group on European aid. And Taylor agreed also to participate in a similar group being set up by the National Planning Association that included representatives of labor, agriculture, and the professions, as well as businessmen among its members.

While these groups worked away on the problems, the battle for public opinion was being waged largely under the impetus of the Committee for the Marshall Plan. Headed by elder statesman Henry L. Stimson and former Secretary of War Robert P. Patterson, this group of more than 300 prominent figures carried on an extremely energetic and effective campaign.

By the end of the year, the Gallup Poll was registering a strong tide of public opinion toward support of European recovery and even Senator Taft was disturbed by the reports he began receiving from party workers across the country on the adverse effect his blunt isolationist stand was having on his presidential aspirations.

However, with the national election only months away, the question of who would control the power and the patronage that would go with such massive appropriations was an issue of such central importance that it became the central factor in determining the final outcome.

Republican supporters of the program generally tended to favor giving the funds to a corporation with an independent board of directors that would clearly be free from the control of the Democratic administration. Various versions of such an approach were outlined by such spokesmen as Winthrop Aldrich, Alfred P. Sloan, and by Lewis H. Brown, Board Chairman of Johns Manville. The Democrats, on the other hand, wanted to keep the entire function within the Department of State, if possible, and in any event under the direct supervision of the Secretary of State.

Hoffman saw clearly how completely the economic issues were intertwined with the political power struggle. And fortunately, Raymond Rubicam with his interest in political economy and Wayne Taylor with his long experience in government and finance, shared his perception.

Both the CED and the National Planning Association groups worked through the winter, concentrating on the issue of "effective administration" of European recovery. In February, 1948, each group released its report and recommendations. Although the CED report also dealt with the economic aspects of the European Recovery Program, both were in significant agreement on the "general principles and administration" of the program.

Congress, that is, the Republicans, should determine the broad basic policies governing the program and should delegate precise powers for their execution to the President, that is, the Democrats. A new administrative agency should be established to be headed by an administrator directly responsible to the President, that is, the Democrats, but appointed with the very real advice and consent of the Senate, that is, the Republicans.

The administrator and his key staff people should be appointed from among the "large number of able men who served our country during the war and gained fruitful experience with questions similar to those presented by the program of cooperation." This, clearly, was a reference to the businessmen, most of whom were Republicans, who had so largely staffed the wartime production agencies. Moreover, there should be a special U.S. Ambassador "to facilitate the operation of the program in Western Europe as a whole," who should be responsible equally to the administrator (Republican) and the Secretary of State (Democrat).

This is the administrative formula that was made public as the Senate Foreign Relations Committee conducted its hearings on the bill. And it was the formula that was in the Economic Cooperation Act of 1948 when Senator Vandenberg rose before a packed Senate on March 1 to present the bill with the unanimous endorsement of the Foreign Relations Committee.

Nevertheless, the debate in both Senate and House was vigorous and prolonged, but it was passed by substantial majorities and became law on April 3.

Having been largely responsible for writing the practical political compromise on the administration of the Plan into the law, Senator Vandenberg was determined to see it carried out in practice. President Truman's initial choice for administrator was Undersecretary of State Dean Acheson, but the latter urged the President to engage in "real consultation" with Senator Vandenberg on the appointment. He told the President that he thought the Michigan senator would propose Paul Hoffman for that job, and added that he thought the President should agree to the suggestion.

The President, therefore, was not surprised when Senator Vandenberg met his suggestion with the declaration that the Republican majority was expecting that the job would go to a man of broad business rather than governmental experience. Moreover, he pointedly observed, Paul Hoffman's name was at the top or near the top of every list of possibilities that had been proposed. He was confident, he added, that Hoffman's appointment would be promptly and cordially endorsed by the Senate.

President Truman was acutely aware that even though the act had been passed by good majorities in both chambers, the large appropriations needed to implement it must still be voted. The entire intent of the act could be frustrated by inadequate provision of funds. To get these, he needed Republican support in general and the active help of Senator Vandenberg in particular. In addition, he knew and he liked Hoffman and had followed CED's policy statements with interest. Some eighteen months earlier, when inflation had been his major preoccupation, it was Hoffman and George Harrison, president of New York Life, whom he had called in to advise him. He had appointed Hoffman and a sizable segment of his CED colleagues to the Harriman Committee and he was not unaware of the closeness, or the importance, of the relationship that had developed between the

Studebaker president and the Michigan senator. Thus it was, only six days after the Economic Cooperation Act became law, that Paul Hoffman was sworn into office as administrator.

Swiftly the Republican Hoffman chose as his deputy in Washington, Baltimore industrialist, financier, and Democrat, Howard Bruce. For the ambassadorship to head the operation in Europe, Hoffman proposed to the President that he appoint either Lewis Douglas, the President's Ambassador in London, or Averill Harriman, his Secretary of Commerce, both Democrats. Harriman was chosen, and William C. Foster, Republican, was named as his deputy.

Foster had worked closely with Hoffman in CED and had written its policy statement on meeting the needs of small business. But he was only the forerunner of a long list of CED associates that Hoffman swiftly swept into ECA jobs. Wayne Taylor, Edward Mason, Calvin Hoover, and Richard Bissell were among the first contingent that scattered into hotel suites and hurriedly arranged temporary offices to begin constructing the new agency.

The political realism that lay behind the administrative play greatly assisted Hoffman in obtaining the services of the businessmen he wanted. There was another undercurrent running strongly in his favor. Many of them confidently expected that their service with ECA was merely the training ground for the bigger jobs that would be theirs when a Republican administration took over after the November election. By the time the electorate sprang its surprise, however, most of them were so caught up in the importance and excitement of their tasks that the defections were few and replacements were quickly available.

Thus it was that out of economic chaos abroad and political confusion at home there emerged one of the most successful and significant adventures in foreign policy in American history. The forces at work to produce this result were complex and numerous. As Senator Vandenberg told the Senate in his historic

March 1 address, it was "the final product of eight months of more intensive study by more devoted minds than I have ever known to concentrate on any one objective in all my twenty years in Congress."

Most students of the event agree, however, that a crucial role at a decisive hour was played by the combination of sound economics, practical politics, and knowledgeable public administration represented in the reports of the National Planning Association and the Committee for Economic Development. And, as *Business Week* observed at the time, "it was Hoffman's CED work more than anything else that made him a national figure" and the leader of the great adventure.

TEN

Freedom Has Its Price

As THE postwar reaction to liberalism set in, the Economic Club of Detroit heard an important industrialist declare that Paul Hoffman, Eric Johnston, and Beardsley Ruml were three of the most dangerous men in America.

This lightning bolt was no isolated phenomenon. If it was a tribute to the dynamism of the men, it was also the reflection of an increasingly ominous intellectual climate. Senator Joseph McCarthy of Wisconsin had not yet swept luridly across the political heavens, but such a responsible public figure as Senator Robert Taft that same year did not hesitate to brand such a dedicated public servant as David Lilienthal as a dangerous Red.

In this atmosphere it is not surprising that the intellectual probings and ceaseless activities of the group which Hoffman headed as well as Hoffman himself should become lightning rods for the friction that came increasingly from the far right. This was the case even though the motivation for Hoffman's evangelism was his conviction that the private-enterprise system could and should be kept humming at a new and profitable rate.

One writer has given this picture of him at the time:

"Working tirelessly, writing and delivering speeches by the score, taking a short six or seven hours of sleep, and playing poker and bridge with his competitive zeal less often, Hoffman brought to the leadership of CED the same conscientious administration which he had already demonstrated in the reorganization of Studebaker. . . . American industrial leaders found in him the warm heart and mental energy they needed. . . . He had the habits of a Puritan and the stamina of an athlete, seldom taking a drink and never smoking. He put people immediately at their ease—and put them to work. Everywhere he declared that 'the primary responsibility of a businessman is to operate his business profitably.' But, he added, 'to operate profitably there was need for bold planning.' "

This bold planning, not just for business but for the American economy as a whole, would not have seemed so bold had it not been for the long record of timidity in business thinking. But it had created enemies and their antagonism was expressed in charges that CED was too far to the left. This was a charge difficult to maintain, no matter where center might be in one's thinking. But one Wall Street publication went so far in utter misinterpretation and general misquotation of a CED publication as to accuse CED of being communistic.

It was Paul Hoffman's inclination to brush such charges off as too ridiculous to dignify with recognition or answer. He expressed his attitude in this statement to his colleagues:

"I think it is very important that we as a group think of ourselves not as right, left, conservative, or radical, but as *responsible*. What we are trying to do is to get at the facts about the way this economy functions, to face the facts and then go down the roads indicated."

This was sufficiently radical doctrine, however, that by the beginning of 1947 CED's trustees felt that the attacks upon it warranted some form of attention. Out of this concern emerged a reaffirmation of faith in private enterprise that is remarkable on two counts: first, that it was felt necessary to issue it at all; and second, as a succinct expression of enlightened business philosophy. It declared:

"We in CED believe in a free competitive capitalistic economy. We are opposed to any measures which are a threat to its continuance and development. We recognize that there is a need for voluntary joint action, but when such action is undertaken either by government or private groups, the one most important test of that action should be whether it contributes to the stature of our people as members of a free society.

"We believe that the dynamic progressiveness of our American economy must be strengthened to be preserved. We hold that the key to further progress lies largely in constantly increasing our productivity—greater output per man-machine-management hour. We are confident that this goal can be achieved through technological advancement and cooperation between individual management and workers.

"We recognize that the nation is still faced with the problem of developing a sound body of economic policy which will contribute toward the maintenance of productive employment at high levels in a free society. To accomplish this measures must be sought and found which will protect and enhance the natural dynamism of the economy and minimize its tendencies toward prosperity peaks and depression valleys. CED's research program is directed toward this goal.

"We emphatically deny that we are foredoomed in the future to the boom-bust cycle of the past. Any thought that we can have a free economy which will never fluctuate is, of course, nonsense. But we are convinced that this economy of ours can achieve a combination of progressively higher living standards, relative stability, and freedom of choice that will make it the most desirable type of economy in the world."

This platform also had its internal significance for CED. The trustees were beginning to consider the future status of the organization as the self-imposed grace period of eighteen months to two years of continued operation that was imposed in 1946 was running out. And the discipline of defining a philosophy had an important bearing on the decision that had to be made.

There was, of course, some sentiment for closing up shop. A minority of trustees still felt that CED in 1946 had abrogated its agreement with the National Association of Manufacturers and the U.S. Chamber of Commerce and should now make amends by dissolving. But experience was against their argument. Too many businessmen were convinced that the mysteries of economic ways should continue to be probed through the interaction of scholars and businessmen.

The process had, through five years of trial and error, hardened into definite form. It meant, first, thorough analysis of the unsolved problems of the whys and wherefores of business fluctuations and economic growth. This, of course, could be done only by fact-finding; and the small research staff with its protected freedom of approach to any problem, and the Research Advisory Board of outstanding social scientists, with its guarantee of academic freedom, had perfected the methods of free inquiry. The second step, the sifting of these facts, was the cooperative work of the scholars and the businessmen who had, through many painful sessions, done so much to mend the once-broken link between business and economic theory. Their microscopic scrutiny of the carefully gathered data led to the final, most important, and in many ways most dangerous stage— the interpretation of the scrutinized facts and the formulation therefrom of policy recommendations for general economic guidance. And for this final hazardous step, the businessmen assumed full responsibility.

George Harrison, chairman of the Board of the New York Life Insurance Company, headed a group of fifteen, appointed by Hoffman, to make a thorough investigation of the aims and purposes of CED, its place in the business community, and its potentiality for future service to the economy. It unanimously voted to put CED on a permanent basis. When Harrison's report was laid before the trustees at their semiannual meeting in May, 1948, one of the most widely attended meetings in CED's history, there was not a single vote against it.

The decision was made in the face of the necessity to obtain a new chairman, because only one month before Paul Hoffman had plunged into his task as head of the Economic Cooperation Administration. The trustees chose as his successor, W. Walter Williams, who was later to become head of the Citizens for Eisenhower movement and Undersecretary of Commerce, but who was then the chairman of Continental, Inc., a Seattle mortgage banking, insurance, real estate, and property management firm. He was carefully chosen for the chairmanship in spite of his oft-repeated modest assertion that "they were scraping the bottom of the barrel when they found me." A man of engaging manner, voluble and persuasive, the Iowa-born banker had served as president of his home-town Chamber of Commerce and Rotary Club and had been named Seattle's "most useful citizen" in 1946. His only national experience had been as chairman of the President's Conference on Fire Prevention, as president of the Mortgage Bankers' Association of America, and as a director of the International Y.M.C.A.

Walter Williams' comparative obscurity was one reason for his choice at this time. It was felt by many trustees that CED would serve its quiet purpose as a research and educational organization better if it were not headed by a prominent and possibly politically minded businessman. Thus Jesse Jones's old dictum was again followed. After all, Paul Hoffman had not been "famous" when he was drafted to head CED in 1942. Williams' sound business reputation and his proved organizational drive had become well known to CED's trustees during the war when he had done an outstanding job in preparing the Northwest's industrial and commercial communities for postwar conversion. Perhaps because he had started his career as a high school teacher of chemistry and had got into the banking business only by chance, he had found his association with CED a challenging intellectual stimulus and had followed its research program with interest, although he had not participated in it in any way. In later years he was to compare his involvement with the CED

process, after he became chairman, with a postgraduate course in
economics and often pointed to himself as a product of the educational process which Hoffman and his friends had envisioned
on the University of Chicago campus before World War II, and
which CED had become.

Williams knew that he faced a difficult task. Not only was he
following in the footsteps of a most dynamic personality, but
also it was an election year and both political and economic
lightning were crackling in the sky. For the next two years he
devoted nearly all his time to CED's affairs. During the first of
these two years he acted as his own chief administrative officer,
making his headquarters at the New York office. Week-ends
would see him flying to Seattle to attend to his personal and
business affairs. Monday would see him back in New York. He
made, in this time, nearly two hundred talks to audiences all over
the country. At the end of the first year he persuaded an old
Seattle friend, Wesley F. Rennie, to give up his post in Geneva,
Switzerland, as general secretary of the World Y.M.C.A., to
take the post of Executive Director.*

He was helped by the fact that, as an organization born under
Democratic auspices but composed in a great majority of Republicans, CED had always leaned over backward to avoid even
the outward appearance of being politically partisan. From the
beginning it had stressed its nonpolitical and nonpartisan status
and its published statements had led to little valid criticism on
this score. Not only had those who had striven to write national
policy statements achieved a remarkable freedom from personal
bias, but they had also managed to put aside political predilections in arriving at their economic verdicts. It was for this reason
that CED's utterances generally were received with respect if
not agreement. The CED trustees were not unaware of the
importance of their position as spokesmen for a large and growing segment of the business community. They were equally

* During the first year he had the administrative assistance of Mrs. Elizabeth
Harrison Walker, then the corporate secretary of CED.

aware that they had done much to restore business to respectability throughout the country. In public life perhaps no one was more impressed by this than President Truman.

What of the other candidates? Well, Senator Taft had looked at CED with considerable suspicion from the beginning and had clashed openly with it during the legislative battle over the Employment Act. CED was too liberal for his taste, domestically, and especially now in foreign affairs. Senator Vandenberg and Governor Stassen, according to Paul Hoffman, "had the highest regard for CED." Whether they subscribed to all of CED's fiscal and monetary policies as then enunciated is doubtful, but they were impressed by the composition of its membership and appreciative of its serious intent. While Governor Dewey was not on record as having expressed himself on the subject, it was generally believed that, of all the candidates, he was inclined to be closest to CED in his economic thinking.

Of course, as it turned out, the economic predilections of the Republican candidates proved to be of much less significance, and the day when Washington could be taken over by what most businessmen fondly referred to as "a business administration" was postponed for four more years. Whistle-stopping across the country, talking across back fences to disgruntled farmers, and whaling the lobbies and Big Business with old-fashioned "give-'em-hell" zeal, Harry S. Truman became President in his own right.

As long as he stayed in office Truman was always ready to turn the guns of his invective upon the NAM, which he used as a symbol for all that was old and musty, or worse, in the business community. However, he most particularly, and also many of his close advisers, apparently read the dicta of CED with kindly and discerning eyes.

The fact is, neither party dared quarrel with the objectives the trustees of CED adopted in determining to continue the life of the organization. These objectives, which have appeared in every major publication since 1948, declare it is the purpose of the group:

1. To develop, through objective research and discussion, findings and recommendations for business and public policy which will contribute to the preservation and strengthening of our free society, and to the maintenance of high employment, increasing productivity and living standards, greater economic stability, and greater opportunity for all our people.

2. To bring about increasing public understanding of the importance of these goals and the ways in which they can be reached.

All these objectives were to be put to severe test in the decade to follow, which saw a continuing cold war, a shooting war in Korea, the penetration of outer space, a fateful struggle to win the uncommitted nations of the world, two minor business recessions, the spread of inflation, an unprecedented boom, and, in early 1958, what some erroneously feared was the beginning of the first dangerous depression since the 1930's. But in 1949, the businessmen of CED placed the issue of personal liberty ahead of economic problems in their priority list of preoccupations.

"A disturbing sense of insecurity is everywhere," the Research and Policy Committee declared in a policy statement, *National Security and Our Individual Freedom*, issued in December, 1949, which remains to this day a readable and provocative document.

"The imminent threat of war will rise and fall; we may face alternating periods of optimism and pessimism; but the threat may last for decades. We must assume that war is not inevitable but we must also assume that there is little prospect of genuine peace in the near future. Large-scale measures for national security seem necessary for years to come."

From this realistic and prophetic introduction, the statement went on to warn that the security program resulting from this situation would affect the lives and freedoms of individual Americans in many ways.

"It is reflected in peacetime selective service. It is reflected in the loyalty investigations. It is reflected in high and still higher taxes and their effect upon our behaviour. It is reflected in censorship over scientific and technical information. It is reflected in the confusion of citizens unable to evaluate national policy because of limited knowledge and information."

The great increase in the role of the military in government, in bureaucracy, in the dominance of government over business and industry, and in interference with individual freedoms, might well lead to what the CED statement called a garrison state. On the eve of McCarthyism the committee warned: "We already have given up important freedoms without adequate challenge. Freedoms unexercised may be freedoms forfeited.

"This trend, particularly if coupled with fear and hysteria or with complacency and ignorance, may produce policies which, in the name of security, endanger essential liberties. Security measures, uncurbed by the requirements of freedom, can undermine our free institutions. Public apathy and pressure for security can lead us along a dangerous road. . . . In the name of security, channels of information dry up; the press becomes a mere purveyor of official handouts. . . . The process of public discussion atrophies. Political parties decline. The power of Congress dwindles. . . . The courts weaken. Cut off from information, the power of the citizen fades. Local plans are subordinated to central purposes. The free market is constricted. Labor is hedged in by special regulations. Consumers find their range of choice reduced. Decisions come to be made by an all-powerful government. All freedoms suffer."

Much of the statement was directed toward the workings of the National Security Act which CED widely criticized while at the same time offering suggestions for its improvement. Among other grave matters then disrupting America's defense machinery, CED was deeply concerned with what David Lawrence (whose *United States News & World Report* reprinted the policy statement in full) called "the tragic differences that have arisen at the top levels in Washington between the armed services."

Among its recommendations for alleviating this situation CED urged that "within the Department of Defense there be a strong civilian staff independent of control by the military services to aid in developing and evaluating defense policy." This, of course, was said at a time when the armed services were still in the process of "unification." CED did not think that any one man, meaning a Secretary of Defense, should be the only civilian control over the services.

Although it did so indirectly, CED in 1949 hit upon a serious problem that was to reappear late in 1957 when America was beginning to recover from the shock that stunned her by the appearance of the Russian "moon" in the skies, while United States moons and even rockets were still earth-bound. In the confusion that followed in the fall of 1957, Senator Ralph Flanders of Vermont, the old CED warhorse, was not alone in his belief that "the millions we have appropriated and spent (on the missile program) on service rivalries, on committees and subcommittees, on advisory committees and subcommittees, on channels of communication up, down and sideways in the trackless maze of the pentagon" had been most improperly used. Nor was he alone in suggesting that "the management of scientists, engineers, and military experts" be placed in the "competent, authoritative" hands of a civilian.

Although the realism of CED's statement is still apparent in regard to our military establishments and our scientific achievements, the underlying importance of the document is that in 1949 an outstanding and respected organization of business leaders took time off from its fiscal and monetary worries to tell Americans that in one vital segment their government was not facing up to one of the most profoundly disturbing social and political problems of the day. For in its insistence upon freedom CED was striking at the heart of the matter. There were two ways to do this, as the *Christian Science Monitor* said. "One is to do it like . . . crotchety old men who are displeased because the world is going through a revolution. Another is to do it as has CED . . . with perspective, comprehension, confidence, and eloquence, too."

Although the statement freely conceded that security must take "temporary precedence" over freedom in time of war, it stated flatly that "at the present time, the balance must be weighed in the direction of freedom.

"Freedom itself, and the self-discipline necessary to freedom, contribute to security," the statement said. "Freedom of scientific inquiry contributes to the production of improved weapons. The maintenance of a free economy encourages the development of economic strength and the growth of a strong, self-reliant people. The maintenance of individual freedoms creates the greatest bulwark of our security—the energy and intelligence of free men working together to build and to save their own and their country's freedom.

"Even more important, freedom and the dignity of the individual are the very foundation of our society, and the ends for which we are striving. Without them, security loses its purpose."

Korea and the New Fight for Stability

THE NATION moved into the second half of the twentieth century witnessing, as Thomas B. McCabe put it, "what the economy may be like as it functions under more normal postwar conditions."

The calm was soon to be completely shattered from far-off Korea, but the Republican Chairman of the Federal Reserve Board was already engaged in a major battle of mounting intensity with Secretary of the Treasury John Snyder over the independence of the Federal Reserve System in handling the control of credit.

President of the Scott Paper Company until President Truman had appointed him to the key post in the nation's central banking system in 1948, McCabe went to Washington with the reputation of a supersalesman. His quiet, soft-spoken charm, reflecting a Quaker background, supported this impression. But he was steadily proving himself to be a tough fighter with an intimate knowledge of the weapons of finance.

Although he had started as a salesman for the Scott Paper Company a year after graduating from Swarthmore in 1915 and had moved up steadily in the ranks of that company, he was no stranger to finance. Since 1928 he had been a director of the Federal Reserve Bank of Philadelphia and had been chairman of that regional bank since 1939. He was the kind of man Jesse Jones wanted to have in the Committee for Economic Development. He had been one of the group's most active and dedicated trustees, but it was clear that in 1950 he still felt the business community needed more education about the nature of the economy.

"I cannot emphasize too strongly," he told the Joint Congressional Committee on the Economic Report, "the difficulties we are placed under when many of the most vociferous supporters of free enterprise, businessmen and bankers, and their organizations criticize the possession and use by the Federal Reserve System of necessary authority over the cost and availability of credit as if the delegation of this authority to the System were characteristic of a 'managed economy' or an 'administered state.' It is exactly the opposite."

McCabe received eloquent support for his point of view from at least one banker, J. Cameron Thomson, president of the Northwest Bancorporation of Minneapolis. The volatile, self-educated, articulate Minnesotan was chairman of the CED subcommittee on monetary and fiscal policy, and with succinct brilliance he placed before Senator Paul H. Douglas's committee the essence of CED's stabilization policy. The subsequent adherence of the Douglas committee's report to CED's line of thinking marked an important step in the development of a national consensus on this general economic policy. It played an important role in the feud between the Federal Reserve and the Treasury and alleviated much of the confusion that followed the outbreak of war in Korea and that continued to spring out of the struggle for political power in the elections of 1952.

The brief but cogent report of the Douglas subcommittee was directed toward determining the effectiveness of coordinated monetary, credit, and fiscal policies as methods of attaining and maintaining high and stable levels of employment and production. Much of the thinking of CED's statements since 1947 was incorporated in this able report.

The gist of the Douglas report lay in its assertion that the major method of general economic stabilization should be reliance upon monetary, credit, and fiscal policies because these are most consistent with the "maintenance of our democratic system and with the fostering and promotion of free competitive enterprise." These instruments "do not involve the Government in detailed control of the particulars of the economy; they do not require the Government to intervene in individual transactions between buyer and seller, in dealings between employer and employee, and in the determination of the prices and production of particular commodities. These millions of intricate decisions are left to the operation of the market mechanism while general monetary, credit, and fiscal policies work toward stabilization by influencing the total supply and cost of money income at the disposal of the private sectors of the economy. There is every difference between the effects of general over-all monetary, credit, and fiscal policies which indirectly influence the economy toward stabilization and the effects of an elaborate system of direct controls.

"Those who would oppose using monetary, credit, and fiscal policies for stabilization purposes, either by refusing to give the Government adequate powers or by obstructing its use of these powers, must therefore either oppose the purposes of the Employment Act or find other methods of equal effectiveness and of equal compatibility with our democratic, free-enterprise system," the Douglas committee said.

As CED had often pointed out since first setting forth its stabilizing budget policy in 1947, it was impossible to say with precision how effective a stabilizing device a vigorous and coordinated use of fiscal, credit, and monetary policies would be. There was little in our past history to help in making such an estimate, because a timely vigorous and coordinated use of all these policies for stabilization purposes had never been seriously attempted in this country. It was soon to be put somewhat to the test.

"Fortunately, however, the validity [of this device] does not need such a precise estimate," the Douglas report continued. "It is enough to know that these methods can be very powerful and that they are preferable to other methods for promoting economic stability. We do, however,"—and here the report again echoed CED warnings—"wish to make two points with respect to the effectiveness of these instruments: (1) They are not a panacea for all economic ills, nor do they make it unnecessary for us to use wise economic policies of other types; . . . and (2), if not used in a coordinated and supplementary manner, the various components of monetary, credit, and fiscal policies are likely to prove insufficient to cope with strong cumulative forces which at times create depressions and at other times inflation. . . ."

The willingness to use them, even more than the theories themselves, was put to severe test just a few months later with the Communist invasion of Korea. The war broke on an economy that was operating at full speed. There was little slack in the labor market. Steel was producing at more than 100 per cent of its rated capacity. The fiscal picture featured what was regarded as high tax rates, an unbalanced budget in boom times, and a large public debt. It was natural that inflation, controls, and taxes became issues as portentous as our setbacks at the fighting front.

The conflict between Snyder and McCabe was one of the first to flare up. Ever since 1927, when Andrew H. Mellon had successfully asserted the supremacy of the Treasury Department over the intended independence of the Federal Reserve, the nation's central banking system had subordinated its credit control activities to the Treasury policy of seeking a low interest rate on the public debt. But on August 18, a new era exploded.

After the government securities market had closed for the day, Secretary of the Treasury Snyder announced he would exchange 13.6 billion September and October maturities for thirteen-month notes bearing an interest rate of one and one fourth per cent. One hour later, the financial world was shocked by a definite declaration of independence by the Federal Reserve Board. It announced an increase in the discount rate of the Federal Reserve Bank in New York from one and one fourth to one and three fourths per cent, and laid it on the line that it was prepared to use all the means at its command to restrain the further expansion of bank credit.

The anti-inflation-minded Federal Reserve had wanted credit tightened up and felt that while the "easy-money" policy might save the taxpayer interest money on the public debt, it would cost him more by inflating the price of what he bought. But the Treasury Department had opposed this line. It wanted no rise in interest rates and it wanted a firm prop under its issues. Heretofore it had nearly always been able to impose its will upon the Federal Reserve Board; but the defiant action of August 18 opened a running battle that was not to be settled until the famous "accord" of March 1951 recognizing the independence of the "Fed,"—an armistice that some looked upon as being at least as significant as that to be reached later at Panmunjom.

It was, however, but one phase of the domestic war against inflation that swirled also around the issues of taxes and controls throughout the entire Korean conflict. Although McCabe's colleagues in the Committee for Economic Development never claimed to be an "economic fire department" they responded quickly to the general alarm that sounded with the Communist assault.

Within two months of that flash of lightning which made "the basic facts of our world situation clearer than they had been before," as it described the Korean aggression, CED issued a special statement called *Economic Policy for Rearmament*. Its authors, Meyer Kestnbaum, Marion B. Folsom, J. Cameron Thomson, John D. Biggers, Gardner Cowles, Fred Lazarus, Jr., Philip D. Reed, and Beardsley Ruml, first took up President

Truman's recommendation for an immediate tax increase of about 5 billion dollars, which would have brought in nearly 3 billion dollars through collections in fiscal 1951.

In the face of the emergency the Committee for Economic Development put aside use of its stabilizing budget policy in its program for rearmament. Although it estimated that the 3 billion dollars in collections would not be sufficient to balance the cash budget, it supported the President's tax recommendations. At the same time it predicted the necessity for another tax increase in 1951. In doing this it recognized the need for speedy action and chose to support the President rather than risk damaging delay.

In its statement CED predicted that military expenditures, which were about 15 billion dollars when the borders of the Republic of Korea were breached by the Reds, would rise to a maximum of 35 billion dollars within a year. This was a fairly accurate guess. The committee knew from its experience on the industrial firing line throughout the late war that American industry had the capacity to carry through the program with only slight reductions in total over-all supplies of civilian necessities. It was sure also that, despite necessary cutbacks in goods using metals or other scarce materials, the civilian stock of durable goods could continue to grow at a rapid rate. It felt that the big task facing the nation was finding ways and means speedily to define and execute a workable program which would achieve necessary military might and industrial efficiency without disturbing the economy.

The great danger was the inflationary potential. Adding some 20 billion dollars worth of extra military demand to nonmilitary demands, which were already near America's productive capacity, "could produce a great excess of demand, with resulting general price increases, unless adequate steps are taken to curb the non-military demands. Inflation would impede the military effort and cause immediate and future hardships to the American people beyond the real requirements of the program. The inflationary potential must be restrained at its source, which is excessive demand."

CED felt there were five steps which, if taken promptly and powerfully, would do this without recourse to price controls, wage controls, or rationing, measures which "inevitably interfere with the process of production and distribution . . . reduce the flexibility and adaptability of the economy, weaken incentives . . . and interfere with the growth of productivity." First, the government should curtail its nonmilitary expenditures to the utmost. Second, it should raise taxes "so that, as the military program absorbs production, taxes will withdraw income from private hands." Third, it should conduct a savings campaign so that through the purchases of defense bonds the public would benefit while supporting the military effort. Fourth, it should take advantage of the continuing large maturities of federal debt to sell more bonds outside the banking system and reduce the supply of money. And finally, it should restrict credit to curtail those demands financed mainly by credit expansion, especially demands for consumers' durable goods, for housing and for business plant, equipment and inventories. It also felt that selective excises at high rates on products using heavy resources needed for military production would be helpful.

Within days of the invasion of South Korea the public, which had no way of knowing how far the Far Eastern brush fire would spread, had started a mad rush to buy up sugar, tires, nylon stockings, food freezers, and other "necessities" before the administration could crack down with rigid controls and a return to ration stamps as in World War II.

The "coordinated and supplementary" use of fiscal and monetary measures was anything but complete. There was uncertainty over the possible duration and intensity of the Korean War and a tendency to assume the best. The 1950 congressional elections made both parties reluctant to face up to the more irritating restraints. Only inflation gained as action on both taxes and controls lagged.

Although it was obvious that taxes had to go up, consideration of the necessity in business circles tended to concentrate on opposition to the proposed imposition of an excess profits tax. Only two voices from the business world called for more taxes or coupled their opposition to the excess profits tax with the presentation of alternatives. One voice was that of Beardsley Ruml's Business Committee on Emergency Corporation Taxes and the other came from Ruml's colleagues in the Committee for Economic Development. Both were strikingly parallel in urging more saving, less nondefense spending, stiffer credit controls, and higher taxes. And both maintained that the excess profits tax was not the best way for government to get at corporate profits, that its inequities, waste, administrative difficulties, and inflationary effect more than outweighed its value in recapturing war profit.

Issued in the fifth month of the Korean War, CED's policy statement, *Paying for Defense*, proposed that a "defense profits tax" of 15 per cent—or more, if the need for revenue should warrant it—be added on top of the basic corporate tax rate of 38 per cent. In addition, it called for a 5 per cent increase in individual net income taxes. Even though it had traditionally opposed most excise taxes, CED called for general increases on the ground that such taxes were a quick way to earn large amounts in an emergency.

CED's program for high taxes, tight credit, and government economy—the monetary-fiscal approach to paying the cost of defense that otherwise would have been met either by open inflation or by suppressed inflation and total controls—received general approval in the nation's press. As one Midwestern newspaper put it, the CED recommendations as a whole made it clear that at least one segment of the business community had "measured the gravity of the situation" and had no inclination to play the "tax tag game" through which profits might hope to escape the burden at the expense of other sources of revenue. Its rugged suggestion for a 5 per cent income tax rate increase and for adding a billion dollars through increased excise taxes (which smacked of a sales tax to some critics) met with little opposition.

The CED approach was too rigorous, however, for the Congress, and a considerably milder bill was passed, including an excess profits tax rather than the proposed "defense profits tax." Then, in December came the entry of the Chinese Communists into the war and the stunning setbacks sustained by the United Nations forces.

"The confident days of the ten per cent war are gone," *Business Week* declared. "The nation faces its greatest crisis. Nothing less than the fate of our country is at stake. Individual citizens who sense the danger must arouse others to action. The hour is very late."

The sense of urgency was felt in CED whose trustees saw the need for increased military spending and for higher taxes to pay for it. So even though their earlier proposals had been rejected as being too rigorous, they were nonetheless determined to face the demands of the mounting budget. In March 1951 CED launched its third attack within eight months on the nation's fiscal needs with these ominous words:

"Taxes are already high. Now we need still higher taxes; higher than we have ever had, even at the wartime peak."

Congressional consideration of the budget for fiscal 1952 was almost as embroiled in the issues of the 1952 election as in the financial implications of the Korean War. And it was in the midst of this turmoil that the business leaders of CED spelled out their rather Spartan tax plan in considerable—and controversial— detail. The great danger, their statement went on to say, was still inflation. Ever since the outbreak of hostilities in Korea prices had been rising. In fact, in the previous eight months they had risen 7 per cent in spite of the imposition of general price and wage ceilings. The budget estimates predicted a 13-billion-dollar deficit for fiscal 1952 that would almost certainly boost them further.

Facing this picture, the businessmen of CED came up with

ways to cut government expenditures by at least 3 billion dollars. But this was just the beginning of a policy. The next step was the hard one to take. Despite vigorous controversy and an unusual percentage of dissent, the committee nevertheless urged increases in taxes to yield an additional whopping 10 billion dollars. Its proposals included an additional 5 per cent on taxable income, a new defense profits tax *on top of* the excess profits tax, excise taxes of 20 per cent on automobiles, and 25 per cent on such items as refrigerators and television sets, and even a 5 per cent sales tax on other items, mainly clothing and household goods.

As might be expected, such a stringent approach brought yelps of dissent, some of the loudest from some of CED's own trustees, and a Kansas newspaper echoed the view heard in more populous areas that the CED proposal was "an evil scheme by stupid men." Most editorialists, however, were impressed with the proposals for heavy corporate taxes but they let the sales tax suggestion go by default.

The debate in Congress continued, obscured by the emotion over the return of General MacArthur. The good news that the government's early estimates of military expenditures had been too high and the estimates of revenue receipts too low was barely noted outside Congress. A tax increase was passed, smaller than that which CED had recommended, but reflecting the proposals of this small group in many major respects.

The general unwillingness to use the fiscal weapon vigorously also affected the course of the indecisive battle that was being waged in another sector of the stabilization front—the control of prices and wages. Not until the shock of the successful Chinese entry into the war was there a wholehearted effort to utilize the powers of the Defense Production Act. Charles E. Wilson of General Electric was summoned to Washington to head the Office of Defense Mobilization and Michael DiSalle was put in charge of price control.

Even as late as the close of 1951, *Business Week* was lamenting that businessmen were showing "little inclination to take mobilization jobs," and were so preoccupied "harboring grudges against the Fair Deal" that they could not sense the national emergency. The magazine cited the case of a company president who refused to give one of his vice-presidents a leave to fill a top emergency defense job in Washington. Somewhat exasperatedly the magazine told business readers that "their stake in who runs controls is tremendous."

The question of price and wage controls had, of course, been a major interest of the businessmen and scholars who gathered together in CED to deal with the problems of World War II, and their concern with this issue had not lessened in the intervening years. In the sixteen months between February 1951 and June 1952, they issued three separate policy statements on the subject.

The effort to impose a major military effort on top of a civilian economy running full tilt had, of course, caused the demand for goods and services to outrun supply. A so-called classical "inflationary spiral" early in the struggle became a real threat to stability.

As a check to this situation Congress, at the administration's behest, had imposed direct controls to stabilize prices and wages. Although CED was fundamentally opposed to any imposed controls except in extreme emergencies, its policy makers took the position that, since the decision had been taken, everyone should do all in his power to make controls work as effectively as possible. Since controls dealt only with symptoms and not with underlying causes, the committee warned that they would "not by themselves stem the tide of inflation."

Instead, it said, they would lead to black markets, to deterioration in the quality of manufactured goods, to distortion of the pattern of production and distribution, to lessening of production of what the consumer wanted, to weakening of competition and efficiency, and to reduction of incentives. The United States was faced with the paradoxical situation of having to find ways to increase production and restrain demand.

It suggested, in a statement issued in February, 1951, certain ways to accomplish the former. These were: to bring women and older workers back into the labor force; lengthen the work week; expand the nation's productive capacity; improve productive techniques; and increase imports from other countries. As to the latter: to reduce nonmilitary government expenditures; raise taxes; check the expansion of bank credit; and encourage national savings.

Toward the end of 1951 the committee elaborated upon its stand on price and wage controls. By this time Congress had extended until June 30 the provisions of the Defense Production Act, under authority of which controls had been made possible. Looking closely at what had been attempted by the administration, the committee found that it had adopted what CED rather scornfully called a "mixed system of controls"—half-flexible, half-frozen, and wholly untenable from CED's theories of sound economic practice.

The committee believed that the only appropriate and workable system would be one best described as a "flexible adjustment system," in which each price and wage ceiling would be initially set but subsequently adjusted to reflect changes in the costs that were relevant to it.

This, of course, CED considered merely as supplementary to sound monetary and fiscal policies and said that it should be designed to restrain increases in price and wage *rates*, rather than profits and wage *incomes*. "The measures devised to carry out a flexible adjustment policy of controls should impose a comparable degree of restraint on the movement of wages and salaries, of farm prices, and of business prices. In so doing it should be the aim of control authorities to avoid discrimination both between these different economic elements and within each economic group."

Furthermore these measures should give incentives to producers to keep down costs and should require some absorption of cost increases for a limited period before passing them on in price and wage increases. The CED policy was designed to slow down and limit, not to prevent, all increases of particular wage and price rates.

"If adequate monetary and fiscal policies are followed," the committee said, "business would not always be able to sell their goods at the ceiling price, and wage earners would not always be able to negotiate increases up to the ceilings on their rates of pay. Except in a period of very sharp inflation, therefore, many prices and wages will be below their ceilings in a flexible system. This would leave large areas of the economy subject to the forces of competition, which stimulates efficiency and the development of cost-saving processes and equipment."

By June, 1952, at a time when the extension of the Defense Production Act was being considered by Congress, CED said flatly that the time for ending all controls had come. It wanted the Defense Production Act to be extended only as far as the end of the year. And it wanted an immediate adoption of a vigorous policy of selective decontrols. The intervening six months, it said, would give the country time enough for an "orderly return to free markets."

Recognizing that a new international crisis might lead to a sudden upsurge of prices and wages, it urged revision of the Defense Act to provide, through joint congressional resolution, presidential authority to impose a ninety-day freeze of prices and wages. During this period Congress would act to determine whether continued controls were needed and what form they should take. It said the National Security Resources Board, which had the authority, should prepare a practicable and equitable price-wage control system for congressional consideration, when and if needed.

But by June of 1952, the question of who should be elected President of the United States in November had become the major preoccupation, and recommendations dealing with fiscal, monetary, and stabilization policy fell upon ears already attuned to campaign oratory and the prospects for new power alignments.

Some months before, McCabe had chided his fellow trustees of CED for what he felt was their lack of responsiveness to public issues. As he put it, when CED was started in 1941 "there was an urgency in the air. It was popular to devote ourselves to public service. We were all serving in the war emergency and we were still haunted by the specter of the Thirties. We wanted deeply, urgently, a better world than any of us had known for our youngsters.

"If we are candid," he bluntly went on, "we will admit that the spirit of intense personal dedication to the public welfare is less acute today. Now most businessmen would prefer to be left alone to pursue their own desires.

"CED must maintain its research," he added, "but it cannot rest on research alone. It also needs a great cause."

For most businessmen, the great cause became the "great crusade" of presidential candidate, Dwight D. Eisenhower.

TWELVE

Business Takes Command

ON JANUARY 20, 1953, Dwight D. Eisenhower was inaugurated President of the United States. The first "business administration" since Herbert Hoover's had taken command in Washington, and if all was not yet right with the world most businessmen were confident that it soon would be.

Hailing the appointment to the Cabinet of those Big Corporation Men, George M. Humphrey and Charles E. Wilson, *Fortune* magazine congratulated President Eisenhower for his "political audacity." In the sixty years since the Big Corporation had moved across the horizon into the foreground of the American scene, the only appointment comparable to these two, *Fortune* declared, was that of Andrew Mellon, and he, "it is well to remember, was immediately made a target of bitter attacks and was still being shot at years after he retired."

Studying the Cabinet appointments made by other presidents in those sixty years, *Fortune* found that ninety-seven had gone to lawyers. Of the rest there had been only thirteen businessmen, mostly small or medium-sized, ten publishers, nine bankers, eight brokers, six self-avowed politicians, six educators, six farmers, four engineers, four Army officers, three labor leaders, two social workers, and one doctor.

"If what businessmen have been saying for the last twenty years has any validity, now is the time to prove it," publisher C. D. Jackson asserted. "We have been given our chance."

"Our chance," he warned, "is not just to make money. Our chance includes a solution in Korea. Our chance includes winning the cold war. Our chance includes winning World War III without having to fight it. Our chance includes progressively solving the social problems in this country. Our chance includes setting such an example, such a center of magnetism to the whole world, that the conquered segments of the Russian Soviet Empire will begin to be drawn off in such a way that disintegration will set in. Our chance includes a dynamic direction of our diplomacy, our trade, and our defense policies toward the single end of world peace and unity."

"If we don't deliver this time," another businessman declared, "we will be back in the doghouse for forty years instead of twenty."

This mixture of rejoicing with responsibility was characteristic of the trustees of the Committee for Economic Development. Although avowedly nonpolitical as an organization, many of its members were close to the inner circles of the new administration.

Had not President Eisenhower himself, during his days on Morningside Heights as president of Columbia University, been a trustee of CED? So also had been Secretary of the Treasury Humphrey; although neither had served on any working subcommittee nor on the all-important Research and Policy committee. In choosing Marion B. Folsom as Undersecretary of the Treasury, Mr. Humphrey took away the organization's national chairman. His predecessor, Walter Williams, had been cochairman of the Citizens for Eisenhower, and now became Undersecretary of Commerce. And Folsom's two successors as chairman of CED, Meyer Kestnbaum and James D. Zellerbach, both subsequently were given appointments in the administration.

Government service was not, however a new experience for the businessmen of CED. Pioneers Benton and Flanders had served in the Senate. High positions in the executive branch had been filled by such men as Will Clayton, William C. Foster, Paul G. Hoffman, Thomas B. McCabe, and Wayne C. Taylor. In fact, although during its first fifteen years the number of trustees never exceeded 150, a total of thirty-eight had held elective or appointive offices in the federal government.

That this group of business leaders was now to play an important role in shaping the economic policies of the Eisenhower administration is unquestionable. This probably was more nearly true in the honeymoon period than it was in the later years. Secretary Humphrey once allowed that the basic thinking of the administration, especially at the time of the 1953–1954 recession, stemmed from *Taxes and the Budget*, the 1947 policy statement in which CED's stabilizing budget policy was enunciated for the first time.

There was, as *Business Week* observed, "a marked similarity between CED and the new administration" that involved more than the names of men. "Both represent the views of a particular type of forward-looking businessmen, a sort of progressive conservatism."

If this new administration, having set lower taxes, a balanced budget, and a stable economy as its major domestic goals, was faced with a challenge so, it might be said, was CED. It decided to get in its licks first. Six days before the President-elect moved his command post from his New York hotel to the White House, a small group of his CED colleagues brought him a carefully prepared nine-page statement of "views on the areas of economic policy most in need of attention."

Meyer Kestnbaum, who had a good reputation for his handling of labor relations as president of Hart Schaffner and Marx and for his interest in education and social work, led the group which included one avowed Democrat, Beardsley Ruml. The others were John D. Biggers, Gardner Cowles, Marion Folsom,

Fred Lazarus, Jr., Philip D. Reed, and J. Cameron Thomson. In what the *New York Times* described as a "cordial meeting," the businessmen stressed to the President the importance of achieving three "basic objectives of national economic policy." These were said to be: provision for national security, promotion of economic stability, and stimulation of economic growth.

Then the group proceeded to present what it described as "five critical requirements" for achieving these objectives. First emphasis was placed upon "a balanced national security program, efficiently executed."

"The American economy can bear whatever burdens reasonable provision for our national security requires," the President was told. "At the same time, security programs that place unnecessary burdens upon the economy, either through error of policy or inefficiency in operation, weaken the national security by weakening its economic foundation."

Expressing confidence that the national security programs "could be more efficiently carried out," the group summarized for the President the proposals first devised by the research and policy group in 1949 for improving the functioning of the National Security Council and the Department of Defense. These proposals called for the development of the National Security Council as the principal executive agency on which the President should rely for formulating and reviewing comprehensive and balanced security policies. To help fulfill this role it proposed that three full-time civilians without other governmental responsibilities be added to the Council. It was also suggested that a Committee on National Security be added to each House of Congress to represent all congressional committees whose jurisdiction covered a significant part of the security field. As far as possible, these two committees should work together in the manner of a joint congressional committee. Subsequent developments indicated that the President was more impressed with those ideas dealing with the Executive than with those relating to the Congress.

Next the group stressed the need for "more effective American efforts to strengthen the economies of other free nations." The business leaders declared that "one of the most vital steps" would be a "fundamental liberalization of U.S. commercial policy," including not only tariff but customs procedures, "Buy America" legislation, shipping restrictions, and loans tied to the purchase of U.S. products.

The third "critical requirement" was the development of "an effective anti-inflationary policy," the President was told. Further inflation would have "very serious consequences," and therefore the cash budget should be kept in balance as long as high employment continued, and the recently won "accord" between the Treasury Department and the Federal Reserve Board should be continued to insure monetary and credit control, flexibly adopted to the intensity of inflationary pressure.

"It is of extreme importance to begin preparations now against the possibility of a depression" at some time during the next four years, the President was told. The major steps that could be taken by government to avert a depression now "are well known." "For maximum effectiveness, these steps must be planned in advance."

And finally, among the conditions for achieving economic growth, "none is more important today than tax reduction and tax reform," the group asserted. When the economies in government spending that the visitors were certain the administration wanted had been achieved, *and* the cash budget balanced, *and* tax reduction made possible, *then* priority should be given to the final dissolution of the excess-profits tax.

The statement was a careful exegesis of the policies arrived at by the Research and Policy committee of CED over the years. Each item in it could be traced back to a policy statement. The concepts of a stabilizing budget policy and the flexible monetary policies, which were at the core of CED's developing philosophy, were clearly discernible. It was, in fact, a program for action by the administration well-fitted to the economic problems of the day. There is reason to believe that the administration studied it carefully.

Ever since 1951 the American economy had been booming. During the first part of this period consumer prices had risen modestly and then, as wholesale prices began to settle down from their Korea peak, they had leveled off. The gross national product rose to the very desirable rate of 4 per cent per year. And unemployment, the real human factor, stayed below 3 per cent of the labor force. During most of this time a "neutral" Federal Reserve System had pursued a hands-off policy.

Then something happened and the boom began to falter. But before this emergency arose, the administration, fearing that inflation was the great threat to stability, set a balanced budget and debt reduction as its major economic goals. This was of course to be expected of a "business administration." Thus there was a considerable flutter of annoyance in the business community (where the annually balanced budget was a shibboleth) when Secretary Humphrey said, soon after the inauguration and while the administration was reviewing the budget inherited from its predecessor, "I don't think anyone can say yet that we can balance the budget, but I hope we won't stop trying."

A shocked United States Chamber of Commerce quickly declared that it would be quite possible to balance the budget without retaining any of the 1951 Korean War tax increases. Furthermore, the Chamber said, it would be possible to balance the budget and reduce the personal income tax by midyear. These two actions, the Chamber thought, should go hand in hand. Meanwhile other tax reductions scheduled by law—excess profits and excises—could become effective on the dates planned.

In the midst of this, in a statement entitled *Tax Expenditure Policy for 1953*, CED had this to say:

"We regard the tax expirations and reductions provided for in the excess profits tax and the revenue act of 1951 as a practical, although incomplete, approach to the much-needed reform of the whole tax system, but only provided that Congress makes reductions in expenditures clearly sufficient to achieve a budget balance at high employment." Only when this was achieved should priority be given to eliminating what the Chicago *Tribune*, which did not quite trust President Eisenhower's New Republicanism and which scorned CED's thinking, called "that evil tax"—excess profits.

Thus CED, speaking straight from its 1947 policy statement, and the administration, following its lead, were close together. President Eisenhower was outspoken in a firm declaration that the time was not yet ripe for ending the excess profits tax. Even Senator Taft grumpily agreed. Secretary Humphrey, in an unusual exhibition of reverse lobbying, personally approached the NAM, the Chamber of Commerce, the American Bar Association, and CED, to plead for support of the administration's policy. He told them the people wanted a balanced budget even if it meant continuing an unfair tax. Marion Folsom also talked with businessmen across the country. But neither the Chamber nor NAM would budge.

The *New York Times* summed up the situation:

"For years leaders of these particular business groups [N.A.M. and the Chamber] have omitted no opportunity to proclaim their undying faith in the balanced Federal budget as the cornerstone of a strong and sound economy. Are we to believe that this article of faith contains a proviso, in fine print, that the budget must be balanced by particular kinds of taxes that they happen to like? No one familiar with the views of CED doubts that it detests the excess profits tax quite as thoroughly as do the NAM and the Chamber of Commerce. But the CED has not permitted either its detestation or its zeal for tax relief to blind it to the central issue involved. Because it regards a balanced cash budget to be 'an essential safeguard against inflation' it sees no logical alternative to backing the President."

At this time things began popping in Washington. Republican candidates and orators had made themselves hoarse during the campaign promising that the first thing they would do when they got back into power—even before cleaning up "that mess in Washington"—would be to reduce taxes. Now the President was openly hostile to tax cuts; and Secretary Humphrey was definitely opposed.

The Republicans, however, set out to redeem their campaign pledges through the famous H.R.1—the symbolic tax-reduction bill that the aging Representative Daniel Reed of upstate New York introduced at the opening of the session. This included provision for the excess profits tax to expire on schedule (June 30, 1953) and advanced the date of a 10 per cent individual income tax cut to June 30 from January 1, 1954. The fight was bitter. But in the end Congress overrode Reed and acceded to the administration's demand. Repeal of the excess profits tax was delayed until January 1, and the individual income tax reduction was not advanced. To win this victory Secretary Humphrey had to promise Congress that the administration would oppose any further extension after December 31, 1953. In September, addressing the American Bankers Association, Secretary Humphrey openly avowed that the tax cuts scheduled for January 1 would go into effect.

Secretary Humphrey, then the most influential Cabinet member, was one of the firmest believers in balancing the budget at a lower rate of taxation and expenditures than we have ever had. Walter Lippmann in 1958 said that Humphrey undoubtedly went along with the 1954 tax cut, not because it was a needed antirecession measure, but because he knew that in the forthcoming Eisenhower budget there would be continuing cuts in federal expenditures. There was, however, a good precedent for tax revision downward: in President Truman's day, before the 1948–1949 recession got under way, the Republican Congress enacted a tax cut and passed it over the angry President's veto. This action plus the heavy federal spending which began in 1949 under the Marshall Plan program, was generally believed to be the reason the Truman recession was so short-lived.

The administration had two reasons for its stand on taxes. It was afraid of inflation, and although at this time a recession was already forming, it then saw no need to stimulate consumer and business spending. Also it did not want to lose the reduction in revenues (now generally placed at 5 billion dollars a year) that was involved. In later years Arthur F. Burns, then chairman of the Council of Economic Advisors, claimed that this tax-cutting action was largely responsible for the prompt recovery from the business recession of 1953–1954. The reduction may well have stimulated buying power. But at the time it was not planned for that purpose.

In the spring of 1953, the tremors of the recession being barely discernible, the end of the boom which had begun in 1951 was not recognized as imminent. Perhaps the timing of the turn was influenced by a sudden tightening of the market by "the perhaps too hasty tightening action" of the Federal Reserve System and the Treasury in the spring, but it is more likely that the causes lay elsewhere. It is generally believed that the downswing began in August with a cutback in inventories. Also responsible was a drastic reduction of federal purchases for national security. Even before any of this was noticeable, the financial markets had become uneasy. Probably more because of this last reason than because it was aware of the former, the Federal Reserve, in May and June, eased credit through open-market purchases. These were followed in July by a cut in reserve requirements. Once again the proper action had been taken, if not for the right reasons.

The Eisenhower administration, from a CED viewpoint, had got off to a good start. But by late autumn and throughout the winter it was running scared. We now know that the recession was characterized chiefly by its mildness. Although the gross national product dropped 1.3 per cent on an annual basis, personal income did not stop rising. At the consumer as well as at the wholesale level, prices remained virtually unchanged. But there was no way of knowing in those uncertain months which way the wind was going to blow. Robert Donovan, in his *Eisen-*

hower, the Inside Story, has revealed that President Eisenhower and most members of his Cabinet, including George Humphrey, were nervous men. Was their wall of prosperity about to come tumbling down? Was the first business administration in twenty years about to become the victim of a business depression—and be driven "back into the doghouse for another forty years"? These questions haunted their meetings.

There was in their discussions a "muting of emphasis on balancing the budget," Donovan has revealed, and even Secretary Humphrey said "a broad public works program would be desirable if operations then in progress should fail to turn the tide." But he still had faith that they would not fail. As soon as the tensions relaxed he and the administration quickly returned to the balanced budget as the great goal.

In his *Economic Report* issued in January, 1954, the President had set forth four principles to be followed: (1) to take preventive action; (2) avoid a doctrinaire position and work simultaneously on several fronts; (3) pursue measures to foster expansion of private activity by stimulating consumers to spend more and businessmen to create jobs; and (4) to act promptly and vigorously when economic conditions require it. In the main the administration followed these dicta.

When in March unemployment reached 3,725,000, or 5.8 per cent of the labor force, the President was considering legislation to beat the depression. As he said, there was more risk in doing nothing than in doing something. And in retrospect it appears that he acted wisely. By June the administration was able to relax and a month later "the dark clouds were blowing rapidly away in the gusts of new prosperity."

There were many reasons for the recovery. In the *Economic Report of the President* for 1955 they were summed up: Consumers not only maintained their spending at a consistently high level, but reduced their rate of saving. Businessmen kept up their capital expenditures at a high rate and increased the flow of dividends. Builders and real-estate developers stepped up operations. Trade unions "conducted their affairs with an eye to basic conditions and with a sense of responsibility." Commercial banks and other financial institutions amply supplied credit on liberal terms. States and localities expanded school, hospital, and road-construction projects. And "the continuing recovery of Western Europe helped to augment our exports. . . ."

"The Federal Government also . . . influenced the economy in two principal ways," the President's report said. "First, through the automatic workings of the fiscal system; second, by deliberately pursuing monetary, tax and expenditure policies that inspired widespread confidence."

The administration had learned two major lessons in "our latest encounter with the business cycle," the President's report asserted. The first was that "wise and early action by government can stave off serious difficulties later." The other was that "contraction may be stopped in its tracks even when government expenditures and budget deficits are declining, provided effective means are taken for building confidence."

Throughout his report ran the thread of CED's thinking on the many-sided means of combatting economic declines which the CED had been so painfully developing over the years. This was perhaps because of the appearance in March, when the President and his Cabinet were meeting in frequent sessions, of a statement of national policy with the apt title, *Defense Against Recession.*

"It seems only yesterday," the *New York Times* said, "when to raise the question of what should be done in case of a business recession was to divide the majority of the adult population into two reciprocally hostile and irreconcilable camps. In one camp would be found those diehards who advocated a policy of 'letting nature run its course.' The other would be comprised, in the main, of those who were convinced that the country's salvation lay in a Government program of public works."

The CED statement stood apart from both these camps. It advocated as essential in the event of a serious business recession that the federal government accept a "quite large budget deficit" as one of the most effective stabilizers the economy has. Any effort to narrow this deficit through higher taxing and lower spending (a theory, Donovan reports, which President Eisenhower was enamored of, in spite of the animadversions of his economic advisors) "would deepen the depression." On the other hand, such drastic measures as big tax cuts and broad public works programs should be resorted to only in declines that "include a large element of cutback in construction and equipment expenditures rather than in declines largely confined to inventory movements," as the 1953–1954 recession was. "There is danger of doing too little too late."

Besides accepting a deficit the report called for making money "easy" early in a recession (which the Federal Reserve had already done when the report appeared). It urged a speed-up of the system of tax refunds, so that a part-time or jobless worker might collect that same year any overpayment of withholding taxes already paid. (President Eisenhower had recommended this in his Economic Report.) It would change the tax law to permit a two-year loss carry-back for business. (A tax law which passed the House the week before the statement appeared had included this.) It would have the states raise the maximum duration and amounts of unemployment compensation above the 26-week limit and the rates of compensation then mostly effective, and have the federal government set aside a reserve loan fund to aid states whose unemployment funds were nearing depletion. (A bill to the latter effect was then being considered by Congress, but it failed of passage; the neglected issue was again raised in Congress in the late winter of 1958.) It would change the terms and maturities of loans and loan guaranties, chiefly housing credit, to meet the economic situation. (The President had recommended this, too, in his Economic Report.) It said the federal government should be ready to lend money to state and local governments to use in planning public works (also an Economic Report recommendation). And finally it would have the federal government devise for speedy use a plan to extend direct loans to states and municipalities to enable them to put the plans into effect. (On this proposal the Eisenhower administration was skittish, although in the Economic Report it did not actually back away from such a mildly New Dealish proposal.)

The statement also contained recommendations for state and local action: to put aside money in good times for public works needed in the future; revise obsolete debt limits; work out a capital budget of works ready to roll; try central marketing of securities of small subdivisions which have difficulty selling in the capital markets; and to improve, where needed, the benefits, coverage, and duration of unemployment compensation.

For business itself it had advice: Continue to develop new products and improve marketing; keep up sales and advertising budgets; follow a more stable inventory policy as a matter of good business; plan capital expenditures on a longer-term basis; reduce short-term debts so that credit would be good if it became necessary to go to the banks to borrow to keep going. And to the bankers it said, "Don't be too tight-fisted when the economic weather gets cloudy."

But perhaps of greater significance was its major program for a *decline of serious proportions*. This, of course, was taken from the accumulation of its past thinking.

"If a large stimulus is needed from the Federal budget it will have to come primarily from tax reduction" rather than from public works. Should this necessity eventuate, the report urged that the administration seek to agree with congressional leaders on the type of tax cut that should be made and then try to put it through Congress in no more than two months. But should this be necessary, such a tax cut should be considered strictly as an emergency measure and carry a fixed time limit, such as one year.

The administration did not allow itself to be goaded into the type of program CED asserted should be reserved for a deep emergency. Nor did it shy away from the proper use of monetary and fiscal policies with their automatic stabilizers. Thus, in Murray Rossant's words, it confounded those "who assumed that Eisenhower Republicanism was merely Hooverism in a soft collar."

During these hectic months no responsible person, neither Republican nor Democrat, came forward seriously to propose that the automatic stabilizers of the American economy be corrupted by the "perverse discretionary action of raising tax rates in order to avoid budget unbalance." As a result of the built-in stabilizers, reinforced by sound discretionary fiscal and monetary actions, a more than 10 per cent drop in production was not permitted to have any real reducing effect upon disposable income.

So the Eisenhower administration got through its first recession unscathed.

THIRTEEN

Leadership Brings Growing Pains

No HOPES were higher than those of the internationalists who crowded Candidate Eisenhower's campaign train and dominated the speech-drafting typewriters. Part of the great crusade was to be the transformation of the often protectionist and sometimes isolationist Republican Party into the dynamic leader of the free world.

The key role of economic policy in this position of leadership was explicitly recognized by President Eisenhower in his inaugural address. He emphasized that "for all our own material might, even we need markets in the world" and added, "equally, we need vital materials and products of distant lands." The strong contending forces inherent in this field of policy also quickly exerted themselves and, in the State of the Union message that followed shortly thereafter, the President coupled with his call for revised customs procedures and extension of the Trade Agreements Act the caution that such action must be accompanied by "legitimate safeguarding of domestic industries, agriculture and labor standards."

Although the change in tone between the inaugural and the State of the Union addresses was noted, the internationalists continued to glow with optimism.

"The issue of trade and tariffs is politically one of the most hazardous facing the Administration, and could conceivably split the Republican party wide open," *Fortune* magazine admitted in its March, 1953 edition; but it proceeded to develop the thesis that "under the 'traditionally protectionist' Republican party, the United States may now be moving toward a freer trade policy than the traditionally low-tariff Democrats were able to achieve in twenty years of power."

Back of these hopes were some significant changes in the American scene. Broad and influential elements in the American business community that had been nurtured on protectionist ideas were evidencing a real change of heart. While some were admitting grudgingly that "free trade is inevitable," the Detroit Board of Commerce in November, 1952, stated bluntly that free trade was also desirable. Others, like Clarence Randall, president of Inland Steel, J. D. Zellerbach, president of Crown Zellerbach, Warren Lee Pierson, chairman of Trans World Airlines, L. L. Colbert, president of Chrysler, young Henry Ford II, and the still younger Charles H. Percy, president of Bell and Howell, were calling public attention to the overriding importance of an active flow of international trade.

In the mind of more than one American industrialist was the vision of the place in history won by two public-spirited Manchester businessmen, Richard Cobden and John Bright, in leading the battle a century earlier to shift Britain from a protectionist to a free-trade country and the dominant force in the commerce of the world. The drastic change in Britain's position after the drain of two world wars lent cogency to the vision of what now might be done for the United States. Urgency also entered the scene as the threat of financial disaster, which had risen in 1947, 1949, and 1951, loomed before Britain again and brought Foreign Secretary Anthony Eden and Chancellor of the Exchequer R. A. Butler hurrying to Washington in the second month of the new administration.

Chancellor Butler's phrase, "Trade, not Aid," had already

slipped into the current American vocabulary. But more than a slogan was needed. Even such a staunch supporter of the administration as *Business Week*, while applauding the "new initiative" in diplomacy, sharply commented that there were "no plans for parallel initiative in the field of foreign economic policy."

Months before, under the leadership of Gardner Cowles, president of the *Des Moines Register and Tribune* and of the Cowles magazines, the trustees of CED had gone to work on the very problem with which the administration was now confronted. In fact, the report issued just three days before Eden's and Butler's arrival not only set forth recommendations for an American trade policy but also gave a number of pointed suggestions regarding the British economy.

Britain's Economic Problem and Its Meaning for America was neatly timed, but it was more than that. It was the beginning of a sustained effort by American businessmen to develop, in terms of specific regions and issues, a foreign economic policy attuned to the dominant position of the United States in the postwar world.

Although the aid program had succeeded in repairing much of the physical damage of war, the CED trustees conceded that they had "come to see that the economic problems of Europe, Asia, and Latin America are more deep-seated than was earlier recognized.

"The persistent economic weakness and balance-of-payments troubles of the European countries, the division of the world economy by the iron curtain, the continued and growing strength of economic nationalism, the hard problems of economic development in Asia and Latin America—all these persistent difficulties in which our national interests and sympathies are directly involved—have now been more clearly revealed. But," the statement emphasized, "the policies for dealing with these problems effectively are still to be found."

Stressing that "the strengthening of Britain and of the Anglo-

American partnership must be the cornerstone of American foreign policy," the report rapped both the British advocates of an "independent" foreign policy, which was branded as being "distinctly neutralist," and those American isolationists who doubted that "anything lasting is being accomplished by our aid."

The idea that Britain's economic difficulties were a temporary result of the war was bluntly rejected and policies based on such an assumption were "self-defeating," the report declared. A new approach must recognize two main deep-rooted and complex problems. The first was said to be that the "output of the British economy has not been growing fast enough, nor in the right directions" during much of this century. Extensive analysis was presented to support the contention that the world's foremost industrialized nation which must export or die had been falling behind for reasons in addition to those of war. Continuing internal inflation was spotlighted as the second major problem.

CED's trustees pointedly told their British business colleagues that their whole industrial complex was suffering from "inadequate adaptive ability," and from "restrictionism and inadequate vigor" in the renewal of plant and equipment, in technical innovation and selling. British labor was also told that it "lacks incentive and is interested primarily in protecting job security by restrictive arrangements."

To increase industrial development, especially in export industries, the British were told they should reduce their public investment in less productive sectors and reorient government policies "to promote investment in the mechanical and metalworking industries, particularly in the capital goods sectors, where the best opportunities for exports exist." Until productivity is increased, increases in wages and other incomes and in government social welfare payments would have to be kept "within conservative limits."

As for the United States, we had to assume a large share of the NATO production program to permit more British industry to transfer from military production to greater output of investment goods. We had to liberalize our own commercial policy to open to the British "the largest and most rapidly expanding national market in the world." Also, an increased outflow of American development capital to the less developed countries, and particularly those which were members of the British Commonwealth, would also be required.

The last recommendation, the report admitted, required further study. Attention was concentrated on "the American tariff and other protectionist commercial policies of the United States." These policies, the report asserted, "were designed for a period, not so many years ago, when the international economy was functioning well, when there was no iron curtain, when the competitive strength of foreign industry relative to American industry was much greater, and when the world was less dependent on American exports." But today, the document contended, these policies reduce the ability of other countries to earn the dollars they need to pay for American exports, tend to keep them dependent on American aid, and thus "add substantially to our tax burden and lead to a less efficient use of our resources."

Cowles's committee therefore urged further reductions in tariffs through an extended Trade Agreements Act "free of weakening legislative amendments such as the 'peril point' provisions; simplification of customs procedures; progressive removal of import quotas on agricultural products, and liberalization or outright repeal of the Buy American Act."

Although these five recommendations seemed to accord with administration policy, they were to be the center of a long and sometimes bitter struggle that promised for many months to make a prophet of the pessimist. This is not to suggest that the CED report was an isolated document. Four days after its release, the Public Advisory Board for the Mutual Security Agency filed a report warning that unless the United States purchased more goods from overseas its "own exports will decline and American industry and agriculture will be seriously affected." And on April 29, the Chamber of Commerce of the United States called for a tariff policy based on broad national interests rather than on the welfare of single industries and advocated outright repeal of the Buy American Act.

The Chamber's action, too, was timely, as it followed soon after the Eisenhower administration's first decision in the Buy American field, one that had sent shivers down the backs of all those who had felt the administration was committed to expanding trade. Secretary of Defense Charles E. Wilson decided against awarding an Army contract for power equipment for the Chief Joseph Dam project to a British firm whose bid was nearly a million dollars lower than the lowest American bid. Also, the President had nominated for an unexpired term on the Tariff Commission former Representative Joseph Talbot, who had voted against the reciprocal trade agreements program in the House and was an avowed advocate of higher tariffs.

These actions led *Business Week* to the plaintive comment that "the internationalists are beginning to wonder just where Eisenhower does stand." Their worries were not lessened by the testimony of Cabinet members before the House Ways and Means Committee on the extension of the Trade Agreements Act. Secretary of State Dulles promised that no new major trade agreements would be negotiated under the one-year extension that was proposed, and he even hinted that the administration might go along with higher tariffs a year hence, after our Allies were prepared for the shock. Secretary of the Treasury Humphrey promised to impose countervailing duties on Uruguayan wool tops. Secretary of Commerce Weeks refused to advocate lower trade barriers and asserted there was merit in the restrictionist Simpson bill which had become the center of opposition to the administration's proposal. In fact, only Mutual Security Administrator Stassen made a clear plea for a more liberal trade policy.

American businessmen attending the Vienna Congress of the

International Chamber of Commerce in May had planned to push the Europeans toward convertibility of currencies and lower trade barriers but instead found themselves on the defensive before European apprehensions over the trend of American commercial policy.

Nor were the defensive and offensive positions—either at home or abroad—altered substantially a few weeks later when President Eisenhower obtained from the reluctant Congress a simple one-year extension of the reciprocal trade agreements legislation which had its roots in the Roosevelt administration. The battlefield merely spread from Capitol Hill to include the special commission on foreign economic policy which Congress had authorized in voting the extension. The seventeen-member commission, composed of five senators, five House members, and seven others, including the chairman, who were appointed by the President, took its name from that of its chairman, the industrialist Clarence Randall.

The hearings conducted by the commission were an extended parade of special-interest pleading, relieved by an occasional demonstration of a broader approach. The National Confectioners Association, for example, argued for higher tariffs for candies but complained of subsidies and duties which raised the price of nuts, fruits, and other ingredients of the finished product. A pulp and paper industry spokesman offered a protectionist program which he admitted had remained unchanged since 1922. Textile firms, bicycle makers, soft-coal producers, wool growers, the glassware and pottery industries, toy makers, watch and jewelry manufacturers were among the petitioners for continued protectionism or for even higher tariffs. Some came before the commission backed by weighty briefs and extended studies. The study prepared for the Synthetic Organic Chemical Manufacturers Association was said to have cost its members more than $150,000. The National Electrical Manufacturers Association, embracing such giants as General Electric and

Westinghouse, presented a study on the growth of foreign competition done by the National Industrial Conference Board.

The debate was enlivened in November by the resignation of the Monsanto Chemical Company from the National Association of Manufacturers in protest against the liberal trade policy speeches of NAM President Charles Sligh. In reporting the event, *Business Week* reported a wag as saying, "It's the first time that anybody ever resigned from the NAM because it was too liberal." But to Monsanto, as to others in the chemical industry, it was serious business and it pursued the logic of its stand by resigning also from the U.S. Council of the International Chamber of Commerce.

It was in this atmosphere that the businessmen and educators in CED decided that they, too, had an obligation to pursue the issues that had been raised in the policy statement on Britain's economic problem and which were now involved in this broader national debate.

This time the study committee was headed by Howard C. Petersen, hearty, vigorous lawyer-turned-banker. He had earned a reputation as an outstanding trouble shooter as right-hand man to Secretary of War Robert P. Patterson throughout World War II and then was Assistant Secretary of War from 1945 until August, 1947. Instead of returning to his successful New York law practice, as he had planned, he ended his government service upon being asked to be executive vice-president of the Fidelity Philadelphia Trust Company. Soon thereafter he moved into the presidency of the Philadelphia bank. There, too, his reputation for swift problem solving and intellectual agility and toughness spread. These qualities and the fact that he had no previous commitments on the tariff issue made him an ideal "new look" chairman. The fact that he had also been an early and leading supporter of the Eisenhower candidacy was no handicap.

Although endowed with exuberant energy, he still looks back on this assignment as an exhausting experience. Even after his subcommittee had reached agreement on a draft, there was vigorous debate in the larger Research and Policy Committee and the subcommittee was told to come back again with a revised draft. While this additional work was going forward, Petersen also personally called on many of the most vigorous spokesmen for the protectionist viewpoint to hear their arguments and to outline the thinking that was developing in his own group. He got, he said, "a thorough dousing" of the opposition viewpoint. So there was the authority of personal experience when he appeared before the Research and Policy Committee the second time with his group's revised report and opened his presentation by saying:

"Gentlemen, if you approve the draft statement before you it will probably cost CED the resignation of several of its most respected Trustees and about a quarter of a million dollars in corporate contributions. But we believe these recommendations are in the national interest and that you should adopt them."

There were resignations and there were substantial withdrawals of financial support. But there were fewer than Petersen had expected, thanks in large measure to his advance groundwork. And today, many of the most vigorous opponents who continue to disagree with the findings have returned to participation and even cite this very statement as proud evidence of CED's striving for objectivity.

Petersen was surprised, however, when among the thirty-three members of the committee, only John D. Biggers, board chairman of Libby-Owens-Ford Glass Company, and Ernest Kanzler, vice-chairman of the Universal C.I.T. Credit Corporation, cast negative votes—accompanied by vigorous footnotes of dissent. Nevertheless, there was deep feeling and reality behind the single-sentence paragraph that opened the statement:

"Finding a tariff policy which is in our national interest has never been more difficult or more important than it is today."

More remarkable, perhaps, was the fact that the statement issued in November, 1954 went considerably beyond the recommendations that had been submitted by the Randall Commission in January and which the President had embodied in legislation which he had sent to Congress in April.

Arguing the importance of creating "greater certainty about American tariff policy," the CED trustees proposed that the President's authority to negotiate trade agreements be extended for a minimum of five years and perhaps longer, in contrast to the administration's request for a three-year authorization. Also, they proposed that the scope of the President's authority to negotiate be extended considerably beyond that requested by the President himself. For example, it was recommended that the President be empowered to trade tariff reductions for other trade concessions or for measures that would encourage private investment abroad.

But what editorial writers across the nation called attention to most vigorously was the report's final statement, which asserted:

"As the strongest economic power in the free world, the United States has a special responsibility for liberalizing trade— the responsibility of leadership. The direction which our tariff policy takes will help to determine whether the free world moves ahead to widening markets and expanding production or whether it moves in the opposite direction, toward intensified economic nationalism and political division."

The *Des Moines Register and Tribune* called this "without question the strongest statement in favor of a liberal trade policy made by any general American business organization" and added that it was "an inspiring example of private business taking the broad view of public policy in the interests of the country as a whole." The San Francisco *Chronicle* asserted that such sentiments would not have been voiced by any sizable segment of the business community twenty years earlier and called the report "a mark of the economic maturity and responsibility which business leadership in this country has steadily developed."

Despite the enthusiasm, national policy picked its way through the long-established battlelines slowly, stumblingly, and settled finally for only partial victory. Plans to join the Organization for

Trade Cooperation to facilitate the negotiation of trade agreements were ditched, and in 1955 the administration was ready to hail as a genuine victory a three-year extension of a slightly diluted Trade Agreements Act of 1934 plus simplification of customs procedures. Certainly no great new ramparts were stormed and the bright hopes of 1953 were considerably dimmed.

An increasingly hollow note had crept into the Trade, Not Aid slogan as the tariff battle waged on. The administration gradually had to shift ground on its hope of eliminating most if not all the foreign-aid program. Appropriations had been cut from 6 billion dollars in the 1952–1953 fiscal year to 2.9 billion dollars in the 1954–1955 fiscal year. By April, 1955 President Eisenhower was asking Congress not only to raise the foreign aid appropriation to 3.5 billion dollars but also, in effect, to accept the proposition that foreign aid had become an essential permanent tool of foreign policy for building a stable free world and not simply a means for meeting an emergency.

Petersen and his group moved into the center of this issue with the strong encouragement of CED's new chairman, James D. Zellerbach. After looking at the policy statement issued in February, 1956, Peter Edson, the Washington columnist, reported that the San Francisco manufacturer and the Philadelphia banker—both Republicans—had "joined forces to give the Eisenhower Administration a sharp jab in the tail."

The statement called on the United States government to expand its program of public investment in the underdeveloped countries and to adopt measures that would stimulate private investment. And it stressed that, while the new Soviet tactic of offering underdeveloped countries financial aid and technical assistance underlined the urgency, expansion of U.S. economic assistance was necessary "regardless of what the Russians do."

"The revolutionary transformation through which Asia, Africa, the Middle East and Latin America are now passing will have far-reaching consequences for the security and well-being of the United States and Western civilization," the committee

declared. "More active participation in developing underdeveloped countries is needed not only to protect our vital, immediate interests. It is needed also to help the underdeveloped
countries build the kinds of societies with which the West can
live in cooperation and peace in the long run."

CED set forth an elaborate program for the use of private
capital in forwarding this aim, but it bluntly rejected the idea
that government aid was no longer necessary.

"Even after all practical measures are taken to increase private
foreign investment from the United States and other industrial
countries, it seems probable that most of the shortage of capital
(in the underdeveloped countries) will remain until development has proceeded beyond its present state," the statement
declared, adding that only government aid could fill the gap. It
stopped by indicating in general terms the extent of the gap, but
Chairman Zellerbach was specific in the speech ·he made to
Washington newspaper correspondents the same day the report
was released for publication. A billion dollars a year more than
the administration was proposing, he said, is not "too much to
earmark" for the job. He maintained that such a sum was one a
400-billion-dollar U.S. economy could "take easily in its stride."

The foreign aid debate, of course, went on, and so did the
CED preoccupation with the issue. In April, 1957, an even more
incisive argument was made for increasing foreign-aid expenditures in underdeveloped countries by a billion a year. The
recommendation was made, the businessmen said, "in full recognition of the need for economies in Federal expenditures to prevent inflation, and to permit important tax reductions and tax
reforms."

Especially significant was an analysis of the 57 billion dollars
the United States had spent for foreign assistance grants and
loans between mid-1945 and mid-1956. The breakdown showed
that less than one-fifth of the total had gone to the underdeveloped countries and that out of this 3.5 billion dollars had
been expended for emergency relief, mainly in war-devastated

areas. Another 3.8 billion dollars had been concentrated in the seven countries with which we have large-scale military arrangements—Taiwan, Greece, Indochina, South Korea, Pakistan, the Philippines, and Turkey. This meant that all the remaining underdeveloped countries of Asia, Africa, the Middle East, and Latin America, with a population of more than a billion people, had received less than 6 per cent of the total aid extended during the eleven years. And in the 1955–1956 fiscal year, the program called for allocations to these countries of some 50 million dollars out of a total fund of 5 billion dollars.

But most significant was the argument in favor of a long-term development loan fund. Whole sections from this part of the statement appeared in the congressional testimony of Secretary of State John Foster Dulles. The factual analysis and the arguments in support of a long-term program undoubtedly played an important part in the subsequent establishment of the Development Loan Fund.

At the same time that Petersen's group was calling for the addition of a billion dollars to the federal budget for aid to underdeveloped countries, another panel under the leadership of James F. Brownlee, then a partner of J. H. Whitney, was examining the economic consequences of the defense burden. Their particular concern was the widespread contention, sometimes voiced by President Eisenhower himself, that there was a point at which the economy could be crushed under the weight of defense expenditures, and the cold war thus yielded to the Soviet Union by default. It took over a year more for the Brownlee group to reach a conclusion, but the results when they came were unequivocal.

"We must not hobble ourselves by the notion that there is some arbitrary limit on what we can spend for defense, now within reach, that we can exceed only with disastrous consequences to the economy," the statement asserted. Expressing a profound concern that our defense posture should be kept adequate, that war be avoided and further Communist encroachment be checked, the committee said that the United States can achieve these objectives while continuing the growth of our economy and preserving our basic democratic freedoms.

CED warned that the nation faced a "continuing situation of constant danger with which we apparently must live for many years." And then, the philosophy which had run beneath all its work on foreign economic policy emerged in the pointed declaration that when it comes to the security of the nation "we can afford what we have to afford."

FOURTEEN

Boom, Bust, and the Budget

THE YEARS between 1955 and 1957 were the years of the Eisenhower boom. They also were years in which the fear of a runaway inflation disturbed the makers of policy in and out of the administration. Beginning in mid-1955 wholesale prices began their ascent, followed in early 1956 by steep rises in consumer prices. Gross national product in real terms jumped right after the 1954 recession had ended but advanced only slowly in the next two years. Unemployment on the average registered about 1 per cent higher than in the earlier Eisenhower boom of 1951–1953.

On the theory that the American people had never had it so good, and because of the great personal popularity of the President, the Eisenhower administration in 1956 was mandated by the electorate to keep up the good work. And then, once again, something happened.

In January, 1958, the President presented his Economic Report. "As we look ahead in 1958," he confidently said, "there are grounds for expecting that the decline in business activity need not be prolonged, and that economic growth can be resumed without extended interruption."

Under the circumstances that then prevailed it was a statement

brimming with optimism. For at that moment the business ba-
rometer was down and still falling. For more than a year industrial production had been dropping at an alarming rate. Most of
the important indexes had also taken downward curves. Personal
income, which had resisted the trend longest, had begun to give
way the previous September. The automobile industry had cut
back its production of new models and the steel industry was
limping along at little more than half of capacity. And unemployment was the highest it had been since 1950. At 6 per cent
of the labor force when the President issued his report, every
indication was that it would go much higher before the winter
was ended.*

During the previous year the paramount task had been to
restrain inflationary tendencies. To this effect money rates had
been maintained at a high level and fiscal policies were directed
at restraining inflation. But as the year turned there were unmistakable signs that the country was in the midst of a recession
that might become the most serious of any downturn since the
1930's. The wise use of fiscal and monetary tools was called for
now, if it ever had been.

Most analyses of the situation agreed that the peak in production, employment, and income had been reached in August,
1957. Even at this time the administration had been troubled
with internal dissension over economic affairs. Secretary Humphrey, at odds with the size of the budget, had uttered his famous
warning against a depression that would "curl your hair" and not
long thereafter had resigned. President Eisenhower replaced him
with Robert Anderson, President of Ventures, Ltd., a trustee of
CED, and a quiet, scholarly follower of the school of progressive
conservatism.

* Between August, 1957, and February, 1958, nonagricultural employment
dropped 1.7 million, or 3.2 per cent, and the seasonally adjusted unemployment
rate rose from 4.2 per cent of the civilian labor force to 6.7 per cent. Gross
national product, seasonally adjusted at annual rates, dropped from 440 billion
dollars in the first quarter of 1957, when the economy was operating at high
employment, to 432½ billion dollars in the fourth.

At the same time that business was reducing investment expenditures—which caused orders to equipment manufacturers to fall off, forcing them to reduce production and employment as well as orders to their suppliers—the administration decided that it, too, should cut expenditures. It feared that the upward trend of defense spending would carry outlays far above the budget estimate for fiscal year 1957–1958. It curtailed new contract placements and canceled certain existing contracts, thus bringing about a slight reduction in the actual rate of expenditures. The administration was moved in this direction by a vain hope of remaining within the authorized debt limit.

Although disturbing signs had begun to appear during the summer of 1957, there was a tendency to discount the possibility of a recession and to attribute the signs to the ordinary readjustments of the market place which are forever happening in a free economy. Even when it appeared that the situation was growing serious, there came calm assurances from high places within and without the administration. The recession was really nothing more than a necessary respite for correction among sectors of the economy which had expanded so rapidly they had got out of alignment with each other, said some pundits. They assured the public, which at first was puzzled but had soon grown apprehensive, that the magnitude of any needed corrections was relatively small. They said that the orderly processes of the market economy would surely complete the job of full recovery within a few months.

Although President Eisenhower knew, if he had read his own Economic Report, that "a decline in investment spending seldom lasts only a few months," he was inclined at first to rely on these "orderly processes of the market" rather than upon decisive fiscal or monetary action. The administration, worried about the debt limit, kept expenditures under tight restraint.

Then came Sputnik.

Quickly in its wake came a loud demand for a step-up in expenditures for defense, education, and research. But this demand had no relation to the recession and whatever was done in this respect had little if any immediate practical effect. Federal expenditures for goods and services declined from the third to the fourth quarter of 1957.

The year 1958 dawned and Congress reassembled in Washington to receive the President's new budget, and no overt action had as yet been taken by the administration to encourage recovery. The budget, however, had responded automatically and promptly to the recession. There was acceleration in the rise of transfer payments, especially unemployment compensation. Receipts had declined. The 3.4-billion-dollar surplus of the third quarter of 1957 had shifted to a deficit of 200 million dollars in the fourth quarter.

Those who expected the same prompt and decisive fiscal action which the administration had applied in 1953–1954, when taxes were cut (although, as we have seen, not actually as an anti-recession measure) found little comfort in either the Budget Message or the Economic Report. One searches them in vain for any suggestion of an attempt to use fiscal measures against the recession. By implication, at least, the administration seemed to be relying upon the planned rise in defense expenditures to lift the economy from its slump.

"The proposals of the budget were consistent with this philosophy," one observer asserted. This could be seen in the plans for expenditures on goods and services, "where one would expect to find any reflection of a deliberate anti-recession policy." The estimates presented for fiscal 1958 implied a small decline in such expenditures from the July–December 1957 half-year to the January–June half-year. A rise of about 2 billion dollars in expenditures for goods and services between fiscal 1958 and 1959 was implied by the budget. But this was smaller than the rate of increase that had actually occurred during the preceding years of boom.

This was not the whole story. In the atmosphere then prevailing—an atmosphere not of fright but of deep concern—it would have been possible to forecast a significant decline of revenues. And support might have been found in traditional views for squeezing the expenditures down to these forecast revenues. Indeed, a movement in this direction was considered by the administration, but it was not followed through. Instead, expenditures were adjusted to the level of receipts that might have been expected at a level somewhat below high employment. "What policy underlay this decision is not clear, but it meant that the built-in stabilizers would be allowed to work and no effort would be made to offset them."

Meanwhile on the monetary front the Federal Reserve System took cognizance of the recession. In mid-January it reduced margin requirements from 70 per cent to 50 per cent and then began the first of three waves of reduction in discount rates which, by midyear, caused all Reserve banks to reach a level of 1¾ per cent from the level of 3½ per cent which had prevailed in November, 1957. A month later it announced the first round of reduction in reserve requirements. These resulted in the release of 1½ billion dollars of Reserve balances to member banks. Open-market operations kept the Reserve System's portfolio steady or rising until summer. "In a very full measure," the Federal Reserve Bank of New York later summed it up, "this was a program of credit eases. It was intended to remove, methodically, amply, but not rashly, all of the previous pressures for restraint that had been necessary in times of 'overstretch' when inflation was the dominant problem."

Although in mid-January President Eisenhower had grudgingly admitted that under prevailing conditions a moderate deficit would be preferable to a tax increase, which had been suggested in some arch-Republican quarters, he would not definitely commit himself. A few weeks later he intimated that the administration might favor a tax cut to cope with the recession, thus giving rise to optimism among those who subscribed to CED's anti-recession policies. But the optimism was short-lived. It soon became apparent that the administration was wedded to the position that the recession would take care of itself and not reach levels serious enough to warrant a broad program of public action.

"Let's wait and see," was the watchword.

But from many sides demands for fiscal action became stronger and louder. The administration replied with some marginal measures: orders, for example, to proceed with a defense installation at Minneapolis; a change in procedures for building post offices; an acceleration in the purchase of routine equipment. But none of this made much difference then or later. And so tensions began to mount.

As the recession deepened, the administration did respond with more significant measures. It authorized a step-up in the federal highway aid program. An Emergency Housing Act was passed by Congress. And Congress increased federal pay even beyond the amount requested by the President. An effective temporary unemployment compensation act was passed. And Congress raised defense appropriations above what the administration had requested.

But these were not exactly antirecession measures, except the unemployment compensation act. For all of them there was, as Congress recognized, a wide public demand. Even had there been no recession most of them would have been accomplished.

"Nothing in our economic policy is so deeply ingrained, and so little reckoned with by economists," John K. Galbraith has written, "as our tendency to wait and see if things do not improve by themselves."

Both the economists and the businessmen of CED had long been aware of this tendency and recognition of it was implicit in CED's anti-recession policy, then four years old, in which the prompt and proper timing of definite action was of primary importance. In the middle of the winter of 1958 the long and peaceful accord between the Committee for Economic Development and the administration began to weaken under the economic tensions. An impatience with the administration's policies began to manifest itself.

While a subcommittee was busily bringing to a conclusion its two-year study of the causes and cures of inflation, the irony of which was obvious to all concerned, CED's program committee met in solemn conclave. This program committee was a small subdivision of the Research and Policy Committee entrusted with the responsibility for issuing statements, based on past policy statements, in quick order and in moments of emergency. It was unanimous in its decision to speak sternly now in what its members fully believed was a moment of national economic crisis.

A great national debate had been in progress for several weeks over the possible necessity for a tax cut. That this should be considered at all by leading businessmen was a tribute to the educational prowess of CED which, as we have seen, had been the first business organization to espouse this fundamentally Keynesian concept of fiscal policy. The cutting of taxes was not to be resorted to, in the CED book, "unless the depression became particularly serious," the committee warned. No one could pick up his newspaper in late February or early March without wondering if this time had not arrived. Economists were busy writing letters to the *New York Times*, and poll-takers reported a growing belief in the need for the cure. The administration continued to hope for the best.

The program committee's statement, *Anti-Recession Policy for 1958*, a succinct application of CED philosophy to the current situation, was published on March 23 and immediately attracted attention throughout the nation. It was, as usual, a cautiously worded document:

"The Federal Government can do much to aid in establishing conditions conducive to recovery. By following policies that are helpful now, and by planning for stronger action if it should become necessary, it can assist in maintenance of confidence in the short-run future among private citizens, an essential for resumption of sound business expansion. . . . There is also a responsibility upon government to avoid reacting to the present recession in ways that would impair business confidence, such as extravagant and wasteful spending schemes or new social experiments."

What made it page-one news across the country was its specific proposals for action, hedged though they were with cautious "ifs" and "buts." The indexes of production, income, and employment indicated, the statement said, that by February we had experienced almost as large a decline from the previous peak as had occurred in the recessions of 1949 and 1954. "If the economic situation becomes clearly worse than in the earlier postwar recessions, strong action should be taken." The time to tell would be two months after February. Then if, after allowance for seasonal influences, business activity continued to retract, a tax cut and a speed-up in federal outlays should be effected. The tax cut—unless there was unmistakable evidence of quickly forthcoming improvement—should be a temporary 20 per cent reduction in individual income tax rates, to expire March 31, 1959. The statement said that this would amount to a loss of about 7½ billion dollars to the Treasury but pointed out that it really would be less because the tax reduction would stimulate business activity and hence tax collections. The statement went on to recommend the preparation of an enlarged public works program to be held in abeyance but ready for use if conditions worsened. But it was confident that across-the-board income tax reduction would give the economy the needed lift.

The CED statement was followed by Arthur Burns's advocacy of an immediate and permanent 5-billion-dollar cut in taxes. A little later the Rockefeller Brothers Fund, Inc., was even more Keynesian than the CED statement in its outspoken demand for an immediate reduction in taxes and a rise of federal expenditures.

The reaction within the administration to the CED (and the

other reports) was, to say the least, mixed. Vice President Nixon let the cat out of the bag when he said that the administration had not yet made a choice between tax relief and a major public works program. President Eisenhower, however, had all but ruled out the possibility of the latter when, in a letter to Republican leaders in Congress, he had denounced such proposals as efforts to resuscitate the WPA and other "pump-priming schemes" of the New Deal's 1930's.

The *New York Times* had been loud in its approval of the CED statement. In an editorial which recalled how the administration's anti-recession policies in 1953–1954 "brought to a halt within a few months what many feared would be a deep and prolonged recession and set the stage for a recovery that carried economic activity to the highest levels in the nation's history," it told the President that it was time to "get off center." The next day the President held a press conference.

To those who "blithely," as he put it, say "Let's have a tax cut," he replied that he saw no magic in their proposal nor did he think that a tax cut in itself would restore public confidence.* And so the full and effective use of fiscal policy to meet what everyone else thought was a serious recession, but which he described as "a minor emergency internally," was doomed by presidential ukase. In fairness to the President it must be added

---

* He said: "Listen, there is no courage or any extra courage that I know of to find out the right thing to do. Now, it is not only necessary to do the right thing, but to do it in the right way, and the only problem you have is—what is the right thing to do and what is the right way to do it. That is the problem. But this economy of ours is not so simple that it obeys to the opinion of bias or the pronouncement of any particular individual, even to include the President. This is an economy that is made up of 173 million people, and it reflects their desires; they're ready to buy, they're ready to spend; it is a thing that is too complex and too big to be affected adversely or advantageously by a few words or one particular—say a little this and that, or even a panacea so alleged. So, what I say is: Courage and boldness are very fine things when you know you have got a plan that is really effective, and that is in battle or whether it's here." He went on to endorse the "You Auto Buy Now" campaign which had been explained to him that morning by two Cleveland auto dealers, "really," he said, "a pair of workers."—*New York Times*, April 24, 1958, Transcript of news conference, p. 18.)

that he did not completely divorce himself from the possibility of resorting to a tax cut. He left the decision to Secretary Anderson and congressional leaders "as to when, or if and when . . . we should have to have any tax legislation." But that he was opposed to one is certain.

It will remain for a future historian to explain why the administration did not cut personal income taxes for one year in 1958 as proposed by CED. President Eisenhower did not know, as we now know, that at about the time he was taking his stand against such fiscal action the recession was approaching bottom. Nor did anyone else.

In the CED proposal the committee had predicted that if business activity continued to decline for two months after February seasonally adjusted unemployment would probably stand at 5 million. By mid-May seasonally adjusted unemployment already stood at 5.2 million, compared with 4.6 million in February.

The report also had said that exclusive reliance should not be placed on unemployment statistics, but that nonagricultural employment and production should be considered. The decline of the former was 2.3 million, which meant employment had dropped below the two-month danger line. Gross national product for the first quarter had shown a decline of 18 billion dollars and was clearly declining in April. All reliable indexes showed it might well recede to 24 billion dollars below the peak by the end of the two-month period. Furthermore there had been a steady decline in consumer spending for nondurable goods and services and a drop in personal disposable income, other facts which underlined the need for strong fiscal action.

The CED had said that "it is always possible to find scraps of information, seasonal movements, and signs and portents to rationalize optimism or pessimism as to near-term future events. But they provide no basis for national policy." A survey made two months after the statement was issued, taking these scraps into consideration but paying most attention to capital expenditure surveys, housing starts, new orders, and government spending, gave little grounds for optimism. Instead it plainly revealed that the conditions described in the March program statement as calling for strong action had been met.

In spite of this, no action of a drastic sort was taken. "By the middle of the year," one historian has said, "it was clear that the course of fiscal policy had been strongly influenced by inertia. Apparently little consideration was given to the fact that the effectiveness of fiscal policies may depend on the belief that they will be consistently pursued."

The administration was, perhaps wisely, content to place major reliance upon the workings of the so-called built-in stabilizers, in spite of the fact that unemployment had risen almost to the level usually associated with a serious recession. And it did use monetary policy effectively. The positive steps taken to ease credit—reduction in the rediscount rate and other efforts to make funds available on more favorable terms—undoubtedly were influential in reversing the trend of the economy.

Once again the CED's "defenses against recession" were not given a full trial. Four months after its program statement had appeared the economy had moved swiftly to confound the dire expectations of midwinter. By late spring the decline had ended. By midsummer it was generally agreed that recovery was strongly on the way, if not already at hand. By the end of 1958, one historian had written, "recovery was assured and our economy was on the threshold of new zones of growth and expansion. Abroad, the air had so cleared that, instead of looking inward for artificial methods to support declining markets, the principal European countries were able . . . to widen the convertibility of their currencies, looking outward to conditions of increasing freedom for the expansion of world trade."

But, of course, all was not really well with the economy. In spite of the rapid increase in production during the last eight months of 1958, employment had expanded with exasperating slowness and unemployment persisted at a startlingly high level.

At the end of the year high employment, which CED had

BOOM, BUST, AND THE BUDGET

always placed as the core of a stable economy, was not even
around the corner. Private nonfarm employment was still substantially below the prerecession peak. Unemployment stood at
slightly more than 6 per cent of the labor force as compared
with a little over 4 per cent during the 1955–1957 boom and
about 3 per cent during 1951–1953. Even after accepting the fact
that in recovery employment historically runs slower than
production, the 1958 lag was most pronounced. The enormous
outlays on plant and equipment that had preceded the recession,
with their resultant increase in efficiency and cost-reducing techniques, had apparently brought about a reduction in the need for
production and other manual workers. Automation was here.
Even the demand for clerks and salesmen was less than in the
other two postwar recovery periods. And at the same time the
labor force itself had expanded much less than had been expected. In 1958 it was only about half a million larger than in
1957, although it had been expanding by approximately 1 million
annually preceding the recession.

Such was the unusual fact of the recovery. The unusual fact of
the recession itself had been the price pattern. At the very time
when the unemployment index and other economic charts were
showing that the recession had become more severe than its postwar predecessors, the cost-of-living index was on the rise. Thus
the nation manifested, as those who opposed a tax cut were quick
to point out, the paradox of both recession and inflation at the
same time. And, to add to the confusion, despite the high level of
unemployment, wage rates continued to rise.*

The specter of inflation had long disturbed the thinking of
the Committee for Economic Development. As far back as 1946

* Partly as a result of the automatic increases received by large groups of
workers under long-term contracts containing cost-of-living escalator clauses,
productivity clauses, or provisions for deferred pay increases. "In contrast to
the preceding two years, however, when wage rates rose faster than gains in
productivity could be realized, the 1958 rise in wage rates was probably *less*
than that in output per manhour, at least in many manufacturing lines." (*44th
Annual Report of the Federal Reserve Bank of New York*, 1959, p. 19.)

it had looked upon it with alarm. That year's brief and inadequate study, *Fiscal Policy to Fight Inflation*, had been followed
by others in 1948, 1950, and 1951, in which the dangers of inflation as a permanent fixture of the national economy were
given serious if not conclusive attention.

In 1950 Howard Myers, then research director for CED, had
questioned the adequacy of CED's program to cope with the
unstabilizing forces that he saw developing in the economy. "It
is not certain," he warned the trustees, "that fiscal and monetary
programs can be relied upon to maintain high employment
without inflation in an economy possessing large areas of price
and wage inflexibility." The relationship of prices and wages to
inflation became of increasing concern to the Research and
Policy committee in subsequent years.

Early in 1958 the committee had published a study of economic growth in which the dangers of inflation were seriously
discussed and in which the warning was made that if growth
were to continue one prime policy objective must be to avoid
inflation. This study was especially disturbed by "the tendency
for the wage demands of labor unions to outrun increases in
productivity."

In early summer—when the ink was barely dry on its anti-
recession statement—the committee published the results of more
than two years of intensive study of inflation by a subcommittee
headed by T. V. Houser, then chairman of the board of Sears
Roebuck and Company. *Defense Against Inflation*, while perhaps not the most lucid of CED publications, was an honest and
controversial attempt to get at the heart of what it called one of
the major unsolved economic problems of our time. If the statement left it still unsolved, it made clear that inflation—"an evil
which must not be tolerated"—had become in its opinion the
economic devil of our times.

Its attempts to scourge this devil led it to one important conclusion that was at odds with some of the economic thinking of
the time. It found no evidence to support the widely held belief

that inflation is necessary if the economy is to maintain high employment. The great danger of this belief, it said, was that if not refuted it would lead to inflation as a "permanent way of life in America." Such an acceptance was wrong, for inflation could too easily get out of control. When it changed from a creep to a gallop it would, as all history had proved, cause untold damage to stability and growth.

Looking back at recent surges of inflation (1940–1948, 1950–1951, 1955–1957) it found that the smaller inflationary period of the second Eisenhower boom was the most disturbing. "We were not at war. Our productive capacity had increased greatly. Employment was high. The Federal budget was in balance and the money supply was growing only slowly." Were there new forces at work that confounded the classic definition of inflation? Why did prices rise under such situations?

The report did not quite answer these questions, but if it was unable to determine the causes it was specific in its proposals for cures. If the nation is willing to adopt the proper measures then it can have both stable prices and high employment at the same time, it said. Nor do we have to sacrifice high production to avoid inflation. The only thing we have to do is "to give up . . . the illusion that we can get more out of the economy than we put into it, that we can consume more than we can produce."

To keep this balance is the responsibility of every one, the statement said, but private responsibility is subordinate to governmental responsibility. At all times the responsibility of the government should be "to use its tax, expenditure, monetary, and debt management policies, in combination, to keep the long-term growth of demand equal to but not exceeding the growth of our economy's capacity to produce."

In other words, when demand is growing too fast by this standard, it should be restrained by a combination of monetary restrictions and an increase of taxes relative to government expenditures, or by a decrease of government expenditures relative to taxes. But, when the economy's capacity to produce is in substantial excess of demand, then the government should use its fiscal, monetary, and debt-management policies to encourage a normal growth in demand.

The statement then offered a bold suggestion: the revision of the Employment Act of 1946, with the framing of which twelve years before it had had so much to do. To the objectives of the Act—maximum employment, production, and purchasing power —it would add a fourth objective—stable prices. "Although it is generally agreed that the language of the Act is sufficiently broad to provide the necessary basis for action to keep prices stable, it is our view that it would be worthwhile to write the commitment directly into the Act."

While recognizing that the mere statement of the objective would not by itself produce stable prices, the committee believed a revision would be helpful for three reasons. First, it would "help counteract the view that the commitment to high employment takes precedence over the commitment to stable prices." Second, it "would strengthen the determination of public officials to adopt anti-inflation measures where they are needed." And, third, it would require both the President, in his annual Economic Report, and the Joint Economic Committee of the Congress, in its report on the President's report, to "place greater emphasis on recent and prospective price trends and to discuss in a more systematic manner methods of achieving price stability."

The statement added that aside from the desirability of stable prices the "objectives of promoting economic growth and productivity" should be written into the Act.

The suggestion fell on fertile ground, for in his 1959 Economic Report President Eisenhower said that he would ask Congress "to make reasonable price stability an explicit goal of Federal economic policy" by such an amendment of the Act. This, said Henry Hazlitt, the *Newsweek* pundit who had been over the years one of the most caustic critics of the Employment Act, was the "most important recommendation," for if the "mischievous Act is to be retained this amendment would make it less mischievous, because the Act has been constantly interpreted as a directive to inflate."

On one front the CED statement raised controversy. Even if government succeeds through monetary restraint and tax policy in keeping demand within bounds, it said, prices may still rise because production costs rise. While admitting it had no definite proof, the committee contended that the main cause of such rises was too often the unwarranted demands of labor unions for wage increases.

We do not have "even the beginnings of a public philosophy about the proper limits to the power of labor organizations in an economy basically organized on the principle of competition. Our laws tend to deny the existence of the problem, as if saying that labor is not a commodity changes the facts that labor is the main economic resource and that wage rates are the main element in costs and therefore prices. . . .

"The problem of the proper limits of the character and extent of union power in a competitive, democratic, free society is one that urgently needs objective public discussion. We recommend that the basic laws of the country be reviewed to see whether they permit labor organizations to have a degree of economic power which is not in the public interest."

As might have been expected this recommendation attracted wide and favorable attention in the conservative and business-minded press. But it also aroused much criticism, some within CED itself. Pioneer William Benton, in a vigorous dissenting footnote, summed up the latter when he deplored the tendency of businessmen, now given unwarranted encouragement by CED, to make the "so-called labor monopoly" the whipping boy for inflation. He asked if the 400-billion-dollar rise in plant, equipment, and inventory that had taken place in the past decade might not have been an equally contributive factor. And he deplored, with others, the implication that the nation must have occasional unemployment and recession as a necessary antidote for occasional price instability. Of greater importance, he suggested, was reducing unemployment, or raising employment, and aiming for a 4 or even 5 per cent annual increase in productivity, rather than the 3 per cent that had prevailed for half a century. Do this, he implied, and inflation would take care of itself.

FIFTEEN

Grass Roots and Economic Growth

THE BRIGHT picture of an increasingly prosperous and productive America persistently dissolves into gray blobs as the scene shifts from city to farm. The blobs may change in tone or in size from year to year but the modern American scene has never been without them. They are the dark reminders of an unsolved problem which continues to take a huge toll, in both human and material terms, from American society.

In the last quarter of a century, the federal government has spent over 22 billion dollars on programs to help the American farmer. A similar amount has been spent on related programs, such as purchases of farm products for foreign assistance, of direct and indirect benefit to the farmer although not specifically designed for that purpose. But despite these vast outlays, farm income has continued to decline. The net income of farmers from farming declined 34 per cent from the peak in 1948 through 1956. Because the farm population was declining, income per capita dropped only 6 per cent; but, at the same time for the United States as a whole, per capita personal income was rising nearly 37 per cent.

In 1954, when figures for the previous year revealed that the average net income of all farm operator families was $3,459, including the estimated value of home-produced food, as compared with an average of $6,393 for nonfarm families, the businessmen of the Committee for Economic Development were spurred into action.

"As a group of businessmen deeply interested in national prosperity and productivity," they said, "we cannot ignore the problems of farmers." Their economic position "is a matter of great national concern, both for its own sake and because it is so closely tied up with the well-being of the nation."

J. Cameron Thomson, chairman of the Northwest Bancorporation of Minneapolis, was appointed to head the study. Thomson was anything but the typical banker. His driving energy, his wide-ranging intellectual curiosity, his interest in people and their problems, his enthusiasm for travel, and his seeming inability ever to tire have caused some of his colleagues, with a mischievous eye on his staunch Republicanism, to refer to him as the banking world's Eleanor Roosevelt.

Born of Scottish immigrant parents in Canada where his father farmed and ran a grain elevator before moving to North Dakota and then to Minneapolis, "Cam" Thomson left school after the eighth grade to go to work as a messenger in the Northwest National Bank of Minneapolis. But economic necessity could not quell his desire to learn. At seventeen he began studying nights at a business college and then took courses in banking and economics offered by the American Institute of Banking. Characteristically, within ten years after enrolling as a student, he was national president of the organization. By the time he was thirty-five in 1926 he had become a vice-president of the bank he had entered barely twenty years earlier as a messenger boy with an eighth-grade education. And in 1929 he was a leading figure in the organization of the Northwest Bancorporation, the holding company which now operates 76 banks in seven central northwestern states, and of which he became president in 1933.

He assembled in 1954 a hard-working group of trustees and technical advisers, including among the latter such outstanding agricultural economists as Theodore W. Schultz of the University of Chicago and Oscar B. Jesness of the University of Minnesota. The group studied and debated for two years before it was ready, in January, 1956, to present an *Economic Policy for American Agriculture*. Whereas most businessmen looked upon aid to farmers in terms of their tax bills, the chief lament of Thomson's group was that the expenditures were not achieving results, that farmers were not sharing adequately in the nation's prosperity.

For nearly 2 million farm families, the businessmen pointed out, annual incomes of less than $2,000 are the rule. Many of them are in the cut-over areas of the Great Lakes and the Northwest, but in ten Southern states more than half the full-time farms produce less than $2,500 of market sales a year. In Alabama and Mississippi this was found to be true of more than 70 per cent of the farms.

American agriculture was being victimized by too much production of some farm products, too much instability, and too many low-income families. The report was especially critical of reliance upon price supports because the chief beneficiaries of higher farm prices were the 2 million farm families whose high production accounted for about 88 per cent of all farm products sold; whereas little help was afforded an almost similar number of farm families who sold less than 10 per cent of all farm products raised and whose income was less than $2,200 per year.

"These families produce so little that no feasible increase in farm prices would greatly alleviate their income problem," the group declared, pointing out, too, that price supports also tended to be self-defeating by encouraging excess production.

To deal with the problem of surplus crops, the committee recommended a combination of continued price supports at gradually reduced levels, coupled with a program to pay farmers to take some land out of production. Government rental of this land, primarily wheat acreage, should be geared to bringing production and consumption into balance over a transitional period of perhaps five years.

To deal with the problem of unstable incomes, the committee recommended moderating extreme price fluctuations through a system of flexible price supports or income payments and a storage program. These devices would not be used to affect the long-run movement of prices but would protect farmers against sharp and temporary swings of prices and income.

To alleviate the problems of about 1,000,000 farmers in areas of persistently low incomes, the committee recommended stimulation of what it said were trends already in existence. In the most controversial section and one loaded with political dynamite, it made this daring proposal:

"The movement of people out of farming in the South, where the low-income farmers are largely concentrated, has been more rapid than in the rest of agriculture. This movement should be encouraged by increasing the amount of information available about jobs in urban areas. The possibilities of offering financial aid to families who want to move and of encouraging industrialization in rural areas should also be explored. Farmers who remain in the low-income areas should be assisted in obtaining larger farms; for this, special credit arrangements and training in new methods will be required in many cases."

Even as it had proposed in 1946 the creation of a presidential board of economic advisors and later the establishment of a national monetary commission, so now CED proposed setting up a nonpartisan Agricultural Stabilization Board to determine broad policies and to help protect agricultural policy decision from short-run political demands. The Board would consist of representatives of farmers, food processors, and consumers, serving long terms, staggered so as to provide continuity. It would be headed by the Secretary of Agriculture, function at the policy-making level, and it would report annually to the President and Congress.

To the tax-conscious city dweller, the businessmen pointedly said:

"The costs of whatever adjustments are necessary should be shared by the country as a whole, and not left to be borne entirely by the farmer. . . . There is a moral responsibility on the rest of the economy because some of the most serious present problems of agriculture result from past events in which the rest of the nation shared,"—events such as the forced and unsustainable development of certain lines of agriculture during World War II.

A warning was also added that "we must not try to solve our domestic agricultural problems by dumping and export subsidies, for example, that seriously affect the interest of friendly nations."

The policy statement was widely disseminated throughout the Midwest and other farm areas where it received favorable attention in the newspapers and farm journals. Its suggestion for the movement of small and unprofitable small farmers from the land engendered some rather bitter criticism, but less than might be expected.

Despite the favorable reception, the continuing decline in agricultural prosperity and the continuing failure of public policy stimulated Thomson and his colleagues to reopen the battle in the fall of 1957. An updated and more vigorous presentation of the 1956 policy statement was issued, sharply stating that the government's program was not accomplishing the announced purpose of stabilizing, supporting, and protecting farm income and prices but that instead they were making the farmer's position "increasingly insecure."

Stung by charges that the earlier report indicated a preference for large, corporate farming, the new statement asserted flatly that "the family farm is not vanishing."

"Only 134,000 farms had sales of $25,000 and over in 1954 and the indications are that a large share of these are individually owned and operated. Corporation farms attract attention because in most places they are so rare. The fact that family farms are growing larger is misinterpreted as indicating they are on their way out. Instead they are adjusting to modern technology and modernization. Commercial farming is still overwhelmingly a family business and appears likely to remain so."

Added stress also was placed on the need for special approaches to assist the low-income farmer; and sharp criticism of the administration of the Soil Bank program was accompanied by a strong recommendation that effort be concentrated on retiring whole farms from production, particularly those of marginal productive value. The group then repeated its 1956 recommendations.

Few statements in CED's history received more favorable or more extensive editorial comment. A group of Michigan papers called it "one of the most enlightened, comprehensive reviews of the entire farm social-economic problem seen to date." The St. Louis *Post-Dispatch* asserted the "proposal for the low-income farmers is right to the point," and the Houston *Chronicle* called it "a common sense program for solving the costly and chaotic farm subsidy problem."

The decision to renew the effort for an improved farm program reflected a growing preoccupation with grass-roots economic problems on the part of CED's trustees, born, undoubtedly, of new stirrings within the organization itself. Although not all businessmen had succumbed to what one observer has called the "smuggery of the Eisenhower boom," there was no denying that the somewhat evangelistic zeal of the early days of CED had diminished. A small, hard core of trustees, however, realized that, in spite of good will and friendliness in Washington, there were still major economic problems to be solved. They knew that no matter who might be in power in Washington, the private citizen could not abandon his concern for policy.

One of Meyer Kestnbaum's first acts when elected CED chairman in 1953 had been to appoint an internal review committee to examine the group's entire operations. On the understanding that the group's recommendations would be put into effect, James David Zellerbach, head of the giant Crown Zellerbach Corporation, the second largest paper manufacturer in the country, accepted the chairmanship when Kestnbaum resigned in 1955 to become a special adviser to President Eisenhower. Although Zellerbach's tenure was foreshortened by a presidential appointment as Ambassador to Italy, he effected the recommended changes. Chief among them was a thorough examination by the board of trustees of the need for acquiring new blood and more active members, the creation of the office of president that carried with it membership on the board of trustees, and the election to that office of Dr. Alfred C. Neal. A former professor of economics at Brown University, Neal had been brought in to head up the research work of the Federal Reserve Bank of Boston by Ralph Flanders, and he had risen rapidly to the post of senior vice-president in charge of administration as well as research.

Zellerbach's successor was an unusually apt symbol of the character of CED—a man with equally successful careers in business and in higher education—Donald K. David. When he became Dean of the Harvard Graduate School of Business Administration in 1942, he had behind him an impressive record in business. And when he retired from his deanship in 1955, he had acquired an outstanding reputation as an educator. In "retirement," he had continued his long association with CED, together with such activities as being vice-chairman of the Ford Foundation and a director of such corporations as the Ford Motor Company, General Electric, and the Great Atlantic and Pacific Tea Company.

Under the organizational changes and the new direction, CED took on a new vitality, the lack of which had been more apparent to those on the inside than to the general public and the press, to whom the printed product of CED apparently had remained as authoritative and as exciting as in the past.

In his first speech to the trustees in May, 1957, David asserted, "We must help to develop the potential of hundreds of communities and regions throughout the country to produce more jobs, more productive jobs, and more of the good things of life, for more people.

"Ours is a grass-roots economy," he declared and warned that much of the drag on the nation's economic progress "arises from unsolved problems of local or regional development.

"The barriers to productivity illustrated by areas of chronic unemployment on one hand, and urban growing pains on the other, underscore one basic and crucial fact: the whole field of economic policy on the state and local level is a morass of confusion and neglect."

Spurred by David's initiative, the trustees created a new committee to work on problems of area development and authorized the addition of a new staff division to support their efforts. The first decision was to concentrate on urban-metropolitan problems. The accelerated urbanization and industrialization of the last few decades, said Jervis J. Babb, then board chairman of Lever Brothers and first chairman of the new group, "has produced a new America in which two-thirds of the nation's people, 70 per cent of its industrial jobs, and one half of its real wealth are found in urban concentrations generally designated as metropolitan areas.

"The resulting frictions and economic costs are all too familiar: congestion, urban decay, fiscal incapacities of local units of government, and insatiable demands for schools, water, and sewage plants, and other public facilities."

In characteristic fashion, a group of outstanding experts was assembled to advise the trustees. Research papers to provide grist for the trustees' mill were commissioned. As a start, attention was focused on four problems: (1) the changing economic functions of the central city; (2) the impact of metropolitan growth upon local governmental structures; (3) the scope and effectiveness of community and regional economic analyses; and (4) the scope and magnitude of an effective program of urban renewal.

This concern with the parts of the economic whole also produced a typical eruption from the seldom inactive mind of Beardsley Ruml. After listening to the recommendations submitted semiannually by the dozen social scientists who comprise CED's Research Advisory Board on the national problems needing attention, the familiar Ruml growl was heard saying:

"It sounds to me like you're trying to make this a committee of economists. This is the Committee for Economic Development. And anybody who cares anything about development in this day and age has got to concern himself with the plight of our schools. That is where most of our potential for economic growth comes from."

Ruml received warm support and before the meeting adjourned a group was commissioned to see what could be done to assist in finding solutions for the nation's educational problems.

Actually Ruml's shaft was not as barbed as it seemed. The businessmen he was chiding, as a matter of fact, had long been more than ordinarily interested in the problems of education. Indeed, as a quasi-educational group, a responsibility in this direction had been imposed upon them by the wording of their charter in 1941.

Better economic education in all walks of life, but especially within the business community, had been a major goal of CED from its beginning. It was not until its reorganization on a permanent basis after the war, when the original Field Division was disbanded, that it began to devote itself assiduously to this objective. In 1947 the trustees established what was called the Business-Education committee. The primary objectives of this group, which was to operate for many years under the chairmanship of James F. Brownlee, a New York investment banker, was to extend the CED process of objective research and policymaking beyond its own confines, in an effort to improve economic thinking. After a brief period of trial and error the

Business-Education committee settled upon two programs. One was for the business community itself; the other was for America's public schools, where the state of economics teaching was then, as now, at low ebb.

With the financial aid of the Fund for Adult Education, the committee established a series of College-Community Centers. Within these centers local businessmen and faculty members of local colleges and universities joined in studying economic problems affecting their own communities. From 1947 through 1957 more than 3,000 businessmen participated in some 26 centers. Their efforts resulted in many published studies and reports, several of which attracted national attention. This extension of the CED process, the combining of practical and academic thinking about economic problems, had a stimulating effect in many areas across the country.

Equally stimulating was CED's participation on the educational front line. In 1949 CED was a prime mover in the organization of the Joint Council on Economic Education. This nonprofit and nonpartisan group has since conducted a national program designed to provide better economics teaching where it is most needed—at the high school level. Through a variety of methods, ranging from demonstration classes to television programs, the Joint Council has tried constantly to inspire educational systems to teach economics objectively and as a part of the everyday, problem-solving process in American life.

In 1958, after much study, the CED trustees decided that the Business-Education program needed reorganization along lines that would bring about by trustees and local business leaders in their own localities more consideration of fundamental economic policy issues of concern to CED. It hoped that this concept of its over-all functions would result in wider business participation through bringing to various key centers throughout the country a simulation of the CED process as utilized by the CED itself.

The principal program responsibilities of this committee as established in 1958 are:

Promoting and encouraging among businessmen and other leaders a wider understanding of national, international, and regional economic policy issues.

Promoting a more effective working relationship between business and academic leaders in the analysis and discussion of these issues.

Promoting improvement in the teaching of economics in universities, colleges, and high schools.

To effect the first two purposes the Business-Education committee created what it called its CED Associates Program. This was specifically designed to take to top-level businessmen and educators throughout the country the "unique intellectual experience that has been enjoyed by CED trustees." In order to enlarge the opportunity for discussion, research, and the formulation of economic policy recommendations, and in order to tap new business leadership in the major regions of the country, groups of CED Associates are currently being established in cities where CED trustees are located and are able to sponsor the programs.

SIXTEEN

Money and the Man-Made Moon

FAR OVERHEAD the first man-made moon was in orbit with its taunting tag, "Made in the Soviet Union," flapping in outer space. The American answer to Soviet know-how had not yet reached its launching pad. In Detroit the production lines, those indices of prosperity, were slowing down; and in Pittsburgh the open hearths were cooling off, as the second Eisenhower recession gained momentum. A chill was in the air—a chill of fright over Soviet scientific achievement and of trepidation over the situation on the home front—when the Committee for Economic Development met in Washington in November, 1957, to celebrate its fifteenth anniversary.

The theme of this significant meeting was typical of CED's interest in the current scene rather than in past achievements. Long before the launching of the first satellite the committee's attention had been directed to the growing strength of the "economic offensive" being waged outside the Iron Curtain by the Soviet Union. In its policy statements on national security and on economic development abroad, CED had recognized and discussed this theme. Now the time had come for a broader evaluation of the "threat," dramatized as it was by the launching of Sputnik.

At this meeting five persons well qualified for their task under-took to instruct the assembled businessmen in the true lesson of the Sputnik.* What they said was perhaps best summed up by Chairman Donald K. David: "Behind Sputnik we see a rocket and behind the rocket we see advanced science and technology. However, there is something more behind this. There is a social system of human institutions that, in this case, has made the correct decision about what was important to achieve and has motivated and organized efforts to achieve it."

In the preceding April the committee had warned that there is "no lack of evidence that in the past three years the communist countries have made a major, and effective, effort to expand their economic relations and general contacts with the independent underdeveloped nations. . . . The changed status and aspira-tions of the less developed countries have opened a new broad path of assault upon the Free World by international com-munism. . . . By economic, political and cultural contacts, the communist powers are trying to exploit the ignorance, poverty, physical suffering, and sense of being the world's forgotten people found in the underdeveloped and uncommitted nations of the Free World. Communist success in this field could load the scales of world power materially in favor of Russia."

It was this expansion as well as the increased tempo of indus-trial production within the Soviet Union itself that led Nikita Khrushchev to say in November: "We declare war upon you—excuse me for using such an expression—in the peaceful field of trade. We declare war. We will win over the United States. The

* They were Edward Allen, director of economic research for the Central Intelligence Agency; J. Sterling Livingston, of the Harvard Graduate School of Business Administration; Jerome Wiesner, of the Massachusetts Institute of Technology; W. Warren Eason of Princeton University; and Clarence Randall, special advisor to the President. Their remarks were later printed in *Soviet Progress vs. American Enterprise*, Doubleday & Company, New York, 1958, 126 pp. Omitted from this book were the remarks of Allen Dulles, Chief of CIA, but included was the address of Richard M. Nixon, Vice President of the United States, as well as an address on the same theme by CED trustee William C. Foster, former Deputy Secretary of Defense and co-chairman of the so-called Gaither Committee.

threat to the United States is not the intercontinental ballistic missile, but in the field of peaceful production. We are relentless in this, and it will prove the superiority of our system."

At the Washington meeting, attended by more than 300 businessmen from every corner of the land, the experts took the "declaration of war" seriously. They found the Soviet Union, in many fields besides that of missile propulsion, to be far ahead of the United States. Their documented accounts told of many advances in scientific and technical education, in important fields of scientific, military and industrial research, in the weapons system, in military preparedness. All told, theirs was a frightening picture which put the international economic situation in precarious perspective.

To the business community the revelations must have come as a jolt. In February had not *Fortune*, that great spokesman for the American system, scoffed at the strength of the Soviet economy in an editorial entitled "The Great Swindle?" A month later a writer in *U.S. News & World Report* had called the Russian economic situation "a false façade covering a miserable basic economy . . . 50 years behind the United States" and had asked, "How can one-half of an economy compare favorably with that of the West and the other half be almost non-existent?" And in July the same weekly had summarized Russia as "the world's biggest poorhouse, one of the worst wrecks in history . . . present squalid and future bleak . . . a colossal failure."

Against such smugness the experts at the November meeting hurled sharp and devastating darts. Of Russia's economic strength CED had long been aware, especially as shown in its long-range policy for assisting the economic growth and encouraging the political independence of the underdeveloped nations of the free world. There it had pointed out that those nations where "poverty is widespread and chronic" but where there are "ample resources available for a better life" were the key to the future economic stability of the entire world. The struggle to "capture" the great mass of people living outside the present boundaries of communist domination becomes the great struggle of our time. But important as this problem is, CED was not unaware of the truth of the axiom about first keeping one's own house in order. In his fifteenth-anniversary address Dean David swung away from a comparison of United States and Soviet scientific achievements and social institutions to say: "I want to direct your attention to one of the most fundamental and pervasive of social institutions and to the need for intensive research to make it serve us better. That institution is money. It may seem a long way from money to the man-made moon. But surely that is a mistake, at least in the sense that I am talking about money. I am talking about money *not as an object to be made or saved as alternative to real things, but about money as an instrument that permits the real work of the world to be done.*"

These remarks were by way of introduction to an ambitious and historically important economic adventure. This was the establishment, with the aid of a $500,000 grant from the Ford Foundation, of an independent national Commission on Money and Credit, designed to take the first full look at the public and private monetary policies of the United States that had been undertaken in half a century.* As the *New York Times* remarked, this had all the possibilities of being "one of the most challenging and long overdue basic research projects of our time."

To trace the history of this idea one has to go back to the panic of 1907, a time when the new finance capitalism was establishing itself permanently upon the economic scene. As a result of this upset there was widespread demand for reform. In 1908 the Aldrich-Vreeland Act created a monetary commission which was headed by Senator Nelson W. Aldrich of Rhode Island, the chief representative of banking, manufacturing, and public utilities in the national legislature.

---

* In 1959 the Ford Foundation came forward with an additional $800,000 grant.

For four years this commission investigated any foreign fiscal and monetary system that might offer usable information and, in 1911, after many conferences with leading bankers (including a hilariously secret meeting at a millionaire's retreat off the Georgia coast) presented a historic report to Congress, just as the Taft administration was expiring. Although the new Congress ignored the report, in the end it furnished a later Congress with much valuable data that was used in drafting the Federal Reserve Act of 1913.

The Aldrich plan, which found seventeen major defects in the financial structure, called for a system of currency based on rediscounting commercial paper, a national reserve association, and fifteen regional banks.* Its principal feature was a flexible currency. Most of the leading economists of the day endorsed the plan, as did the American Bankers' Association.

It was published in the same year in which Woodrow Wilson, then Governor of New Jersey, had said "the great monopoly in this country is the money monopoly," a truism that was documented by the sensational revelations of the Pujo Committee two years later, and by Louis D. Brandeis's famous book, *Other People's Money*. Even though many Democrats wanted to follow the Aldrich plan, with a central bank, a currency based on commercial paper, and credit under the control of private banking interests, it fell afoul of William Jennings Bryan, who demanded that the system be placed entirely under government control, and of President Wilson, who felt the same way.

Senator Aldrich died in 1915. The New Freedom, the first World War, "normalcy," and the speculative boom of the 1920's, the Hoover depression, the New Deal, the second World War, the Fair Deal, Korea, two recessions, and the Eisenhower boom—all came and went. And with them vast, almost incom-

---

* Among the most important defects were: the lack of mechanism for mobilizing the reserves of individual banks in times of trouble, a currency system that failed to meet seasonal needs, a narrow money market, and the absence of an organization for obtaining effective cooperation among banks. Most of these needs were met, of course, by the Federal Reserve Act.

prehensible changes in the fiscal and monetary structure of the nation took place.

At the time of the Aldrich report not only was there no central banking system, but there were no guaranteed deposits or guaranteed mortgages; nor were there then any personal or corporate income taxes, group insurance plans, pension funds, or social security system. We were on the gold standard. Installment credit was almost unknown.

In spite of all the changes, neither Congress nor any other public agency had felt compelled to take an over-all look at what they meant, or along what monetary paths they were taking the country. Not only had money and banking laws and practices changed, but there had also been undreamed-of growth in the size of the budget and the national debt, in the government's role as a source of credit, and in the American position in the world economy.

In the postwar years in various political and economic quarters, there had arisen suggestions for making this appraisal. But nothing had been done. In 1948 CED put the idea in tangible form. In a historic policy statement, *Monetary and Fiscal Policy for Greater Economic Stability*, it proposed that Congress set up a nonpartisan commission, with private as well as public members, to delve into the esoterics not only of monetary policy but also of such relevant topics as budgetary policy, debt management, savings institutions, the Federal Reserve System, and international financial policies.

The CED program set forth in broad outline many of the pressing economic problems that were occupying the attention of economists and others at that time,—but 1948 was an election year. There were few politicians who wished to ask too seriously what was wrong with our economic system. Nevertheless, the proposal struck a spark in the Senate where a bill (S.1519), based entirely on the CED recommendations, was introduced by Democratic Senator Maybank and Republican Senator Tobey. It won the unanimous approval of the Senate Banking and Currency Committee. Senator Robertson (D., Va.) brought it to the Senate floor. There was practically no debate and the same afternoon, June 2, 1949, it was passed. In the House, however, it met a different fate. Representative Patman, long an avowed enemy of the Federal Reserve System, saw to it that the bill was smothered in committee.

Later, Senator Paul Douglas's subcommittee of the Joint Economic Committee of the Congress also rejected the CED recommendations because it felt they could better be carried out by a congressional committee than by a mixed commission of legislators and laymen.

In policy statements and in testimony before Congress the Committee for Economic Development was to repeat its proposal several times after 1948. While it met with no immediate result, like many another idea broached by CED, it did not go unnoticed. The Douglas subcommittee recommended a thorough congressional study of the monetary and credit systems of the United States, but even this strong endorsement did not win congressional approval. Nevertheless, the ensuing reports of Senator Douglas's group and of Representative Wright Patman's committee did provide considerable scholarly information that added to the public's understanding of several aspects of the problems involved. In 1956 the American Bankers Association, an advisory committee of the Senate Banking and Currency Committee, and a number of qualified private citizens urged such a study.* But once again nothing happened.

In January, 1957, President Eisenhower, in both his Economic Report and in his State of the Union message, requested the creation of a "commission of able and qualified citizens" which would develop proposals "for the purpose of improving our financial machinery." This idea met with scattered public ap-

* Among them, Elliott V. Bell, publisher of *Business Week*, and S. Clark Beise, president, Bank of America, both trustees of CED, and Allan Sproul, former president of the New York Federal Reserve Bank, who later was a trustee of CED.

proval. Discussion before the Joint Economic Committee and elsewhere in Congress revealed general agreement on the need for such a study—but once again there was disagreement as to who should conduct it. And so—in spite of the obvious fact that our private and public financial institutions had grown so complex as almost to defy understanding—nothing was done.

At this point Donald K. David, chairman of CED, stepped boldly into the picture. He persuaded the trustees to authorize the establishment of a private, independent, national commission on money and credit. As chairman of the executive committee of the Ford Foundation, he got that organization to put forth $500,000 as an initial grant to finance the project. The twenty-five-man Commission on Money and Credit, as it was named, was completely independent of CED. However, it adopted a set of stringent by-laws patterned on the time-tested rules under which CED had built up its sixteen-year reputation for objectivity, independence, and concern with the general welfare. Frazar B. Wilde, who from 1952 to 1958 had been the hard-working head of CED's Research and Policy Committee, became chairman, and H. Christian Sonne, New York banker, CED trustee, and chairman of the National Planning Association, became vice-chairman. The commission began work in 1958. It was not expected to make known its findings for two years.

Mr. David may have been guilty of only slight exaggeration when he said, "I think . . . that such a study will have more impact for the good of us all, in the next decade or two, than the expected advances of knowledge in science and technology. These latter, with their bombs and satellites, will be more dramatic. But increased knowledge in the field of public and private finance may make available a greater source of humanly valuable energy than even potentially exists in atomic energy as such."

As Dean David pointed out, the mere existence of perplexing questions about the efficiency of our money and credit institutions is no proof that the entire system, or even its greater part, is wrong. Even if—as the Radcliffe Commission report of 1959 in England suggested was the case in that country—no major surgery is required, questions have become so widespread that creative answers are needed to prevent harmful changes and inhibitions on proper policy. Even should the commission's ultimate and considered findings result in no immediate legislative or administrative revisions they could, undoubtedly, have far-reaching influence upon the national thinking about money and credit—about "money as the instrument that permits the real work of the world to be done." As a bow to the future economic welfare of the United States, the establishment of the commission was indeed a fitting climax to the first fifteen year history of the Committee for Economic Development.

During those fifteen history-laden years CED, as we have seen, had ranged with a questioning eye over a wide area of economic perplexities, but central to all its concepts was its concern with the economic functions of government and the manner in which they were being exercised. From its inception CED accepted the fact that government was big and was constantly growing bigger and that there was no returning to a simpler, happier past in this respect. It believed that the question was not *how much* government should do, but *what* it should do, and once this was determined how it could be done most effectively.

Thus CED approached the problems with the clear-cut belief that the proper economic functions of government were generally limited to providing for the national security (the cost of which, it insisted, should never be the determining factor), to the raising of revenues, and to maintaining and managing the debt. At the same time it adamantly insisted that government (except in extreme emergencies, such as war) should do nothing to prevent the market from responding to *real* conditions of supply and demand, or to prevent the free reaction of prices, production, and income to the desires of customers (whether individuals, businesses or governments) to buy and to the willingness of suppliers (workers, investors) to produce and sell.

Thus it stood firmly against direct controls over the economy.* Its *bête noir*, of course was price controls in peacetime. But it also waged its war of words against farm price supports, high tariffs, selective excises, the pegging of interest rates on government securities or mortgages, and the support of prices through stockpiling. It rationalized its opposition on the ground that such controls were rigid and arbitrary in their nature and that instead of bringing genuine planning to the market they set up standards inimical to the market's flexible response to the real underlying economic conditions.

This thinking underlay all its policy statements and was at the root of its stabilizing budget policy and its flexible monetary policy, which probably were its greatest contribution to economic thinking in its first fifteen years. But as Herbert Stein, CED's research director, said in a brilliant paper prepared for its trustees: "There is no CED Bible from which one can deduce CED problems now and forevermore. There is only a body of writing, on various subjects and done at various times, reporting the fruits of discussion that is going on and is expected to continue. These writings are steps in a learning process. None is the Last Word."

That the fruits of CED's discussion have been valuable, there can be no question. Nor is there any question that the need for this kind of discussion, at the high level provided by CED through its process of joint academic and business analysis, will be with us for a long time. If any evidence were needed it lies in the figures deduced by Professor Otto Eckstein of Harvard, in a paper prepared for CED, from a painstaking study of the federal budget. In this he showed that, depending upon the spending policies that will be followed in the next ten years by the govern-

---

* Except when in 1958 it suggested that perhaps the time had come for the imposition of what suspiciously seemed to be direct controls over *wage* increases. See *Defense Against Inflation*.

ment, the federal budget will be *from $6 to $34 billion larger* than the 1959–1960 budget, which was the largest budget in history.

In a changing world—with the Communist economic threat on one side and with grave domestic problems ranging from inflation to the deterioration of our central cities—the need for the continuance of the CED process has never been greater. Dr. Stein, in the paper already referred to, has put it most wisely: "If CED's Research and Policy Committee is ever asked to summarize in one sentence what it has done it can say 'We have discussed.' This is not said facetiously or apologetically. Discussion is the distinctive method by which consensus and policy are reached in a democracy. It is the distinctive method because it is the one route through which large numbers of people can unite in action without the use of force. To discuss is the highest duty of the citizen. . . . Discussion is not easy. It is not talk, or brainstorming, or selling, or persuasion. It is the honest mutual exchange of information and opinion. Participants in the discussion must be willing to reveal what they know and do not know, and to listen receptively and critically to the statement of others. *Discussion is possible only among people who are prepared to reexamine what they believe.*"

Appendix

THE ORIGINAL BOARD OF TRUSTEES OF CED

(In accordance with the by-laws lots were drawn to determine the terms of office of each member of the Board of Trustees)

James F. Bell (3-year term)
  (Resigned December 14, 1942; replaced by Jay Hormel)
William Benton (1 year)
W. L. Clayton (3 years)
Chester C. Davis (3 years)
Ralph E. Flanders (2 years)
Marion B. Folsom (1 year)
Clarence Francis (2 years)
Paul G. Hoffman (2 years)
Lou Holland (2 years)
Charles R. Hook (1 year)
Reagan Houston (3 years)
Eric A. Johnston (1 year)
Harrison Jones (1 year)
Charles F. Kettering (2 years)
  (Resigned September, 1944; replaced by William Jeffers)
Thomas B. McCabe (3 years)
Reuben B. Robertson (3 years)

Edgar B. Stern (2 years)
(Unable to serve because of ill health; replaced December 14, 1942 by Harry Scherman)
John Stuart (1 year)
Officers:
Chairman, Paul G. Hoffman
Vice-Chairman, William Benton
Chairman, Finance Committee, Clarence Francis
Chairman, Research Committee, Ralph E. Flanders
Chairman, Field Development Committee, Marion B. Folsom
Director, Field Development, Scott Fletcher

THE ORIGINAL MEMBERS OF STANDING COMMITTEES OF CED

Field Development
Marion B. Folsom, chairman
Chicago—Ralph Budd
Cleveland—George Crabbs
Dallas—E. L. Kurth
Kansas City—Robert L. Mehornay
New York—George Sloan
Philadelphia—Walter D. Fuller

Research Committee
Ralph Flanders, chairman
Chester C. Davis, vice-chairman
William L. Batt
S. Bayard Colgate
Donald David
Max Epstein
Eric A. Johnston
Beardsley Ruml
Charles E. Wilson

Research Advisory Board
  Sumner Slichter, chairman
  Robert Calkins, vice-chairman
  Neil Jacoby
  Harold Lasswell
  William I. Myers
  Theodore W. Schultz
  Ralph Young

CHAIRMEN OF THE RESEARCH AND POLICY COMMITTEE

1942–1946	Ralph E. Flanders
1946–1948	Raymond Rubicam
1948–1949	Philip D. Reed
1949–1950	Marion B. Folsom
1950–1952	Meyer Kestnbaum
1952–1958	Frazar B. Wilde
1958–	T. V. Houser

RESEARCH DIRECTORS

1942–1946	Theodore O. Yntema
1946–1956	Howard B. Myers
1956–	Herbert Stein

CHAIRMEN OF THE BOARD

1942–1948	Paul G. Hoffman
1948–1950	Walter Williams
1950–1953	Marion B. Folsom
1953–1955	Meyer Kestnbaum
1955–1957	James David Zellerbach
1957–	Donald K. David

Statements on National Policy

THE ECONOMICS OF CED

Postwar Federal Tax Plan for High Employment. August, 1944, 47 pages.

Toward More Production, More Jobs, and More Freedom. October, 1945, 37 pages.

Fiscal Policy to Fight Inflation. September, 1946, 21 pages.

Taxes and the Budget. November, 1947, 77 pages.

Monetary and Fiscal Policy for Greater Economic Stability. December, 1948, 60 pages.

Uses and Dangers of Direct Controls in Peacetime. July, 1949, 27 pages.

Price and Wage Controls. December, 1951, 44 pages.

National Security and Our Individual Freedom. December, 1949, 34 pages.

The Threat to Our National Security. September, 1952, 41 pages.

Flexible Monetary Policy: What It Is and How It Works. March, 1953, 35 pages.

Managing the Federal Debt. September, 1954, 38 pages.

Defense Against Recession: Policy for Greater Economic Stability. March, 1954, 53 pages.

Control of Federal Government Expenditures. January, 1955, 30 pages.

Defense Against Inflation: Policies for Price Stability in a Growing Economy. July, 1958, 80 pages.

The Problem of National Security: Some Economic and Administrative Aspects. July, 1958, 61 pages.

CED AND THE POSTWAR WORLD

Postwar Employment and the Settlement of Terminated War Contracts. October, 1943, 15 pages.

Postwar Employment and the Liquidation of War Production. July, 1944, 23 pages.

Postwar Employment and the Removal of Wartime Controls. April, 1945, 31 pages.

Problem of Changeover Unemployment. August, 1945, 29 pages.

The End of Price Control—How and When? April, 1946, 13 pages.

TAXES AND THE BUDGET

Tax and Expenditure Policy for 1949. May, 1949, 45 pages.

Tax and Expenditure Policy for 1950. January, 1950, 51 pages.

An Emergency Tax Program for 1951. March, 1951, 35 pages.

Tax and Expenditure Policy for 1952. April, 1952, 37 pages.

Tax and Expenditure Policy for 1953. April, 1953, 20 pages.

Taxes, National Security, and Economic Growth. January, 1954, 44 pages.

Federal Tax Issues in 1955. May, 1955, 16 pages.

The Budget, The Economy, and Tax Reduction in 1956. June, 1956, 18 pages.

Tax Reduction and Tax Reform—When and How. May, 1957, 39 pages.

The Budget and Economic Growth. April, 1959, 44 pages.

CED AND SMALL BUSINESS

Small Business After the War. February, 1944, 15 pages.

Meeting the Special Problems of Small Business. June, 1947, 59 pages.

CED AND AGRICULTURE

Agriculture in an Expanding Economy. December, 1945, 45 pages.

Economic Policy for American Agriculture. January, 1956, 40 pages.

INTERNATIONAL POLICIES

International Trade, Foreign Investment, and Domestic Employment. May, 1945, 26 pages; includes Bretton Woods Proposals.

An American Program of European Economic Cooperation. February, 1948, 33 pages.

International Trade Organization and Reconstruction of World Trade. June, 1949, 45 pages.

Economic Aspects of North Atlantic Security. May, 1951, 43 pages.

Britain's Economic Problems and Its Meaning for America. March, 1953, 52 pages.

United States Tariff Policy. November, 1954, 38 pages.

Economic Development Abroad and the Role of American Foreign Investment. February, 1956, 35 pages.

Economic Development Assistance. April, 1957, 37 pages.

The European Common Market and Its Meaning to the United States. May, 1959, 141 pages.

MISCELLANEOUS POLICIES

Collective Bargaining: How to Make It More Effective. February, 1947, 24 pages.
How to Raise Real Wages. June, 1950, 43 pages.
Paying for Defense. November, 1950, 43 pages.
Modernizing the Nation's Highways. January, 1956, 25 pages.
Economic Growth in the United States: Its Past and Future. February, 1958, 63 pages.

STATEMENTS BY THE PROGRAM COMMITTEE

(Based on national policy statements of the
Research and Policy Committee)

Economic Policy for Rearmament. August, 1950, 29 pages.
Conditions Necessary for Effective Price-Wage Controls. February, 1951, 8 pages.
Ending Price-Wage Controls. June, 1952, 15 pages.
Tax Policy in 1956. December, 1955, 12 pages.
Toward a Realistic Farm Program. December, 1957, 54 pages.
Anti-Recession Policy for 1958. March, 1958, 22 pages.

Research Studies

Production, Jobs and Taxes. By Harold M. Groves. June, 1944, 124 pages.

The Liquidation of War Production. By A. D. H. Kaplan. July, 1944, 133 pages.

Demobilization of Wartime Economic Controls. By J. M. Clark. January, 1945, 219 pages.

Providing for Unemployed Workers in the Transition. By Richard Lester. January, 1945, 152 pages.

Agriculture in an Unstable Economy. By Theodore W. Shultz. January, 1946, 299 pages.

Jobs and Markets—How to Prevent Inflation and Depression in the Transition. By Members of CED Research Staff. March, 1946, 143 pages.

Financing Business During the Transition. By Charles C. Abbott. May, 1946, 141 pages.

Postwar Taxation and Economic Progress. By Harold M. Groves. May, 1946, 432 pages.

International Trade and Domestic Employment. By Calvin B. Hoover. September, 1946, 177 pages.

Controlling World Trade—Cartels and Commodity Agreements. By Edward S. Mason. August, 1946, 289 pages.

Small Business: Its Place and Problems. By A. D. H. Kaplan. September, 1948, 281 pages.

Monetary Management. By E. A. Goldenweiser. July, 1949, 175 pages.

National Security and Individual Freedom. By Harold D. Lasswell. October, 1950, 259 pages.

American Monetary Policy. By E. A. Goldenweiser. July, 1951, 391 pages.

Stabilizing Construction: The Record and Potential. By Miles L. Colean and Robinson Newcomb. December, 1952, 340 pages.

The Budgetary Process in the United States. By Arthur Smithies. March 1955, 486 pages.

Supplementary Papers

Economics of a Free Society. By William Benton. December, 1944, 6 pages.

Personnel Problems of the Postwar Transition Period. By Charles A. Meyers. December, 1944, 54 pages.

World Politics Faces Economics. By Harold D. Lasswell. January, 1946, 106 pages.

Problems in Anti-Recession Policy. By CED Economists and Consultants. September, 1954, 16 pages.

New Role of the Soviets in the World Economy. By Michael Sapir. May, 1958, 64 pages.

The Changing Economic Function of the Central City. By Raymond Vernon. January, 1959, 92 pages.

Metropolis Against Itself. By Robert C. Wood. March, 1959, 56 pages.

Trends in Public Expenditures in the Next Decade. By Otto Eckstein. April, 1959, 56 pages.

Index